A VISITOR'S GUIDE TO SAVANNAH

by

Polly Wylly Cooper
and
Emmeline King Cooper

Wyrick & Company

Coastal Cities Guidebook Series

Published by Wyrick & Company
Post Office Box 89
Charleston, SC 29402

Designed by Sally Heineman
Printed in the United States of America

Library of Congress Cataloging-in-Publication Data

Cooper, Polly Wylly, 1940 -
A visitor's guide to Savannah / by Polly Wylly Cooper and
Emmeline King Cooper.
p. cm.
Includes bibliographical references and index.
ISBN 0-941711-27-7
1. Savannah (GA.) - - Guidebooks.
I. Cooper, Emmeline King, 1929-
II. Title.
F294.S2C66 1995
917.58'7240443 - - dc20

95-11747
CIP

This publication accepts no advertising. The listings of hotels, restaurants, shops, tourist attractions and other commercial vendors, manufacturers and services are included for information only and do not represent endorsements or recommendations by the publisher.

Names, addresses, telephone numbers, fees and hours of operation were furnished by the owners or operators and were correct as of July 1, 1995. Corrections and additions will be made in subsequent editions.

CONTENTS

ACKNOWLEDGEMENTS

We are grateful to the men and women who have helped us in so many ways. This list includes Emma and Lee Adler, Polly and Randy Brooks, Stephanie Churchill, Robert Cooper, Tim Cooper, Margaret DeBolt, Hector Dewart, John Duncan, V. and J. Duncan Antique Maps and Prints, the Rev. Charles Hoskins, W.W. Law, Jack Leigh, Bunny Lawton, Laura Lawton, Donald K. Martin, Jr., Belinda McLain, George Nichols, Judy and Haywood Nichols, Mary Oemler, Jeanne D. Papy, Callan Pinckney, Lou Poole, David Potter, Hansell W. "Hank" Ramsey, Gail Rountree, Shannon Scott, Esther Shaver, Jenny Stacy, John Thorsen, Henrietta Waring, Ray Wood, and special thanks to our editor and friend, Pete Wyrick.

DEDICATION

We salute the seven women whose courageous action in 1955 was the beginning of the Historic Savannah Foundation, Inc.

1. Katherine Judkins Clark
2. Elinor Adler Dillard
3. Anna Colquitt Hunter
4. Lucy Barrow McIntire
5. Dorothy Ripley Roebling
6. Nola McEvoy Roos
7. Jane Adair Wright

"The Seven" were seared with burning indignation in 1954 when Savannah's City Market was razed to make room for a parking garage. A year later, when the historic Davenport House was threatened with demolition for a parking lot, they banded together to save it just hours before wreckers were slated to begin. And so began the Historic Savannah Foundation, Inc., an organization that is now a model to the world for creative restoration and renovation.

Memories of "The Seven" have inspired us throughout the writing of this book.

BROADCASTING SYSTEM, INC.
ONE CNN CENTER
BOX 105366
ATLANTA, GEORGIA 30348-5366

R. E. TURNER
CHAIRMAN OF THE BOARD

Having grown up in Savannah, I have fond memories of this quiet, ante-bellum, moss-draped city. When I visit, I recall being a "stag" on the debutante scene in the '50s, dancing to Lester Lanin's band at parties hosted by songwriter Johnny Mercer, celebrating Saint Patrick's Day with a few pints of green beer, and having private times to myself—hunting and fishing before dawn at my father's plantation in South Carolina.

The city is, indeed, a national treasure, and Savannahians are rightfully proud of their two-square-mile historic district, which is a Registered National Historic Landmark.

The Historic Savannah Foundation, other organizations, plus many spirited individuals deserve thunderous applause for preventing wanton destruction of classic architectural gems. Through combined efforts, more than 1,100 buildings have been restored.

A staggering seven million tourists visit each year, bringing in over 1/2 billion in revenue.

Savannah is an ideal city for walking. James Oglethorpe, founder of the colony of Georgia, laid out the original four squares as his schematic design for the city. In successive years, this plan was followed until Savannah had 24 squares, plus Forsyth Park.

Springtime finds tourists relaxing on benches in the squares, enjoying the fragrance of flowering magnolia, wisteria, tea olive, pink and white dogwood, and azalea.

I brought my wife, Jane Fonda, to Savannah recently for a bison convention. She thinks Savannah is beautiful!

With Savannah hosting the 1996 Olympic sailing events, it will be stupendous to watch all the activity in the Wilmington River, right in the waters where I learned to sail. I competed in many regattas at the nearby Savannah Yacht Club.

This guidebook, written by my old friend, Polly Wylly Cooper (and her old friend, Emmeline King Cooper), will help visitors discover the same secrets and charm of this lovely city that I experienced in my youth.

Ted Turner

SAVANNAH THROUGH THE YEARS

Oglethorpe's Vision

The year was 1732; the place was London. James Edward Oglethorpe, distinguished soldier and prison reformer at age 36, was urging King George II to sign a charter for a new colony where people "of decayed circumstances" could begin a fresh life. The colony would be called "Georgia" in honor of the king.

Oglethorpe had three strong arguments: the prospect of profits from raw materials; protection for South Carolina from the Spaniards to the south; and asylum for men and women fleeing religious persecution.

Ink flowed from the royal pen on April 21, 1732, as King George lowered his bewigged head to sign the charter for the 13th and last British colony in America.

"Non sibi sed aliis" (Not for self, but for others) was the Latin motto chosen by Oglethorpe and the twenty other men who agreed to serve as Trustees for Georgia.

Next came the task of selecting settlers from the hundreds who volunteered. By early November, 35 families had been enrolled, and Captain John Thomas was readying the frigate *Ann* for a long sea voyage. What a change for young Oglethorpe from a leisured life at Westbrook, his family estate in Surrey, to a leap into the unknown as leader of a shipload of men, women and children, plus hogs, chickens, goats, and geese!

On November 16, 1732, the *Ann* sailed down the River Thames with the town of Gravesend at her stern and new beginnings beyond her bow.

Life Aboard the Good Ship *Ann*

Here are entries from a copy of the ship's log of Thomas Christie, recorder aboard the *Ann*:

"Novr. 24—Wind E.S.E. & E. by N. Moderate & fair...Hazey Wheather & fresh...No Candle to be burnt but in Lanthorn & Ordrd. Mr. Kilbury to go round Every Bodys Cradle & see all the lights put out by Eight. Mist and Lost a black lurching Bitch belong to Mr. Oglethorpe. Supposed to be flung Over board by some of the Sailors.

Decr. 18—Wind East. Fair Whethr...Mr. Oglethorpe caught a Dolphin and being Aprised of some Big-bellyd. Women in the Ship Longing, gave it all amongst them withot. tasting any himself.

Decr. 20—The Long Boat was hoisted out And Mr. Oglethorpe, Dr. Herbert (ship's chaplain) Cap. Thomas, & some Others went a Dolphin fishing wth. fishgig all round the Ship. But undr. an Umbrella, the wheather being very hot."

Oglethorpe Meets Tomochichi

Oglethorpe carried a dream in his heart and a plan in his pocket when land was sighted in February, 1733. With Colonel William Bull of South Carolina, he chose a townsite on a high bluff, 15 miles upriver from the Atlantic Ocean. Living there was a tribe of Yamacraw Indians led by the mico (chief), Tomochichi, who gave Oglethorpe permission to settle the land between the Savannah and Altamaha Rivers, plus several off-shore islands.

From their first meeting, there was mutual respect between the young Englishman and the aged Indian. Oglethorpe even took Tomochichi and the chief's family back to London in 1734 to the delight of the Trustees, as well as King George and Queen Caroline.

During those first days in Georgia, Oglethorpe laid out a plan for Savannah—a grid-like pattern of streets and alleys with house lots and trust lots (areas set aside for public buildings). Central to each of the four original wards on Yamacraw Bluff was an open space called a *square*. Oglethorpe's city plan was faithfully followed as Savannah grew from four to 24 squares. Three squares have been destroyed, but today we can still stroll through 21 of these gracious, green oases here in one of America's earliest planned cities.

Oglethorpe's plan also provided for the Trustees' Garden (near East Broad and Bay Streets), a ten-acre plot set aside to see which seeds, plants, and cuttings would thrive in Savannah's semi-tropical climate. It's said that the first cotton seeds were a gift to Oglethorpe from the Spanish leader, Don Manuel de Montiano.

Many Countries—Many Languages

Then and now, Savannah celebrates its ethnic diversity. Many languages were heard in the Georgia colony, as well as various Indian dialects.

Aboard the *Ann* came Italian Paul Amatis, hired by the Trustees to teach the art of sericulture, or silk production.

Later that year, the *William and Sarah* sailed into the harbor, bringing Jewish settlers. Most spoke Portuguese, and a few spoke German. On board was Dr. Diego (Samuel) Nunes Ribiero, a physician who was invaluable to the colonists in battling yellow fever.

From Salzburg, Austria, came German-speaking Lutherans, exiled by the Roman Catholic Archbishop. Oglethorpe helped them settle nearby at Ebenezer. Slavic accents, filtered through the German language, came with the hard-working, peace-loving Moravians; they arrived in 1736 on the same ship that brought the Church of England clerical brothers, John and Charles Wesley.

Also contributing to the polyglot were French Huguenots and Scottish Highlanders, as well as natives of Switzerland, Greece, Holland, Wales, and Ireland. Even a smattering of Arabic was spoken.

When Oglethorpe's ban on slavery was lifted in 1750, slave traders brought human cargo, adding African and West Indian voices.

Georgia was, indeed, a melting pot, in terms of both diversity and environment, since summer temperatures in Savannah often hung (and still do!) in the 90s.

Bloody Fighting

The Spaniards to the south resented the growing number of colonists in Georgia; Oglethorpe's spies reported that a Spanish attack was being planned.

An early act of aggression took place on board the British ship *Rebecca* when Captain Robert Jenkins had his ear sliced off by the sword of a Spanish sailor. Captain Jenkins was earmarked for posterity when he brandished the pickled article before Prime Minister Walpole, turning stomachs and warming war-mongers. The War of Jenkins' Ear began in 1739 and lasted eight years.

One of the most strategically significant victories of American history took place during this war at the Battle of Bloody Marsh in 1742. While the Spaniards lounged and lunched in a clearing on St. Simon's Island, Oglethorpe and his troops ambushed and attacked, making the salt water run red from casualties that were mostly Spanish. The Spaniards retreated, and King George II awarded Oglethorpe the rank of brigadier general.

Liberty Boys Plot Revolution

Georgia suffered a great loss when personal matters called Oglethorpe home to England in 1743. Back in England, his life took a new direction when he met and married Lady Elizabeth Wright, heiress of Cranham Hall. Oglethorpe's boots never touched Georgia's sandy soil again.

In Georgia the mood was gloomy. Malcontents met and grumbled; the population dwindled; finally, the Trustees relinquished their charter a whole year early.

From 1754 until 1776, Georgia's government was in the hands of a succession of three royal governors. But under the gas lamps at Tondee's Tavern the Liberty Boys gathered, railing against the constrictions of Mother England. Imagine the agony of loyal-to-the-crown James Habersham when his three sons became Liberty Boys. It was young Joseph Habersham who crashed into a meeting in 1776 and put Royal Governor James Wright under house arrest.

On August 10, 1776, the words of the Declaration of Independence reverberated four times through the streets of Savannah; the American Revolution had begun.

Revolution—Recovery—Prosperity

In October, 1779, the American allies waged the Siege of Savannah, an unsuccessful effort to wrest the city from the British who had occupied it earlier that year. Supporting the Georgia patriots were French and Irish troops and black volunteers from Haiti, all under the command of French Count Charles-Henri d'Estaing. The Pulaski Legion was led by the gallant Polish cavalry officer, Count Casimir Pulaski, who was shot from his horse in this battle and died a few days later. This was the death ground, too, of Sergeant William Jasper, whose sacrifice is commemorated by the Irish Jasper Greens militia unit and the monument in Madison Square. Nevertheless, Savannah remained in the grip of the British until the Americans finally triumphed in 1783.

The weight of Mother England had been removed, but still the colony did not prosper. When President George Washington visited in 1791, he had a four-day marathon of ceremony and festivity, but the city was not much more than a straggle of wooden houses on sandy streets.

In 1793, a young man sailed south to Savannah from New York City. His name was Eli Whitney, and his mission was to teach the children of Catherine Littlefield Greene, widow of General Nathanael Greene. Between arithmetic and spelling lessons on Mulberry Grove Plantation, Whitney devised a machine to facilitate the process of combing the seeds from cotton. This invention—the cotton gin (short for engine)—enormously speeded the production of cotton. The city's population (11,000 in 1840) boomed to 22,000 in 1860.

More people meant more houses, and many new houses were built, but of Savannah grey brick and stucco, instead of flammable wood. In fact, because of disastrous fires, wooden construction was forbidden. William Jay, Charles Blaney Cluskey, John Norris, and other creative minds designed the buildings that are the architectural treasure-trove of today. By 1856, all 24 squares were bustling and the green expanse of Forsyth Park had been added at the city's southern border. Yes, Savannah was prosperous, but enslaved hands were turning the wheels of progress.

Moving Toward War

As an agrarian economy grew in Savannah, so did the number of slaves—from zero in 1733 to over 7,712 in 1860.

As more land was planted in cotton, the price of slaves escalated. In 1790, a planter paid $300.00 for a young, healthy male; by 1860, the price was often as high as $1,800.00.

Abolitionists called for an end to slavery, but King Cotton could not survive without slaves to plant, cultivate, and harvest. Savannah in 1860 was busy and bustling, but a terrible conflict was about to begin.

War Rips Families Apart

In November, 1860, Abraham Lincoln was elected president of the United States. In December, neighboring South Carolina seceded from the Union. Here in Savannah, secession fever raged until Georgia, too, left the Union to become one of the

Confederate states.

Early in 1861, Colonel Charles Olmstead and fellow Confederates took possession of Fort Pulaski, in the mouth of the Savannah River. This act brought war even closer.

The war that began in 1861, known both as the Civil War and the War Between the States, was one that both north and south thought would soon be over. But from Fort Sumter in 1861 until Appomattox in 1865, the struggle lasted four bloody years. More than 600,000 were killed and another 400,000 wounded.

Here follows an oft-told story from the *Georgia History Book*, by Lawrence Hepburn:

At the end of a hard-fought battle, after the enemy had fled, a Confederate officer rode slowly over the battlefield. He came upon one of his men carefully digging a grave. Next to the shallow hole, the blue-clad body of a Union soldier was laid out.

"Why are you taking such care to bury a Yank?" asked the puzzled officer.

The Confederate soldier looked up from his work, tears streaming down his boyish face, "He's my brother, Sir."

Picking Up the Pieces

Progress in Savannah after the war was slow, and problems were many. King Cotton still ruled, but because there was little else on the industrial scene, the economic foundation was fragile.

The construction of the Cotton Exchange in 1886 was a statement of trust in the cotton industry, but, in reality, more and more cotton planters were losing their land as prices plummeted. A pound of cotton that brought $1.00 in 1866 was sold for just 7 cents in the 1890s.

Historic preservation was not a focus in those days. Many buildings were lost to deliberate demolition, natural decay, abuse, and neglect. Then came earthquakes, fires, hurricanes, cyclones—a string of devastating natural disasters.

A bright spot in preservation, prior to the founding of Historic Savannah, was the enormously creative utilization of buildings in the Trustees' Garden area, spearheaded in the 1940s by Mary and Hansell Hillyer when he was president of the Savannah Gas Company.

For the most part, Savannah lost luster in the first half of the 20th century. Although much was lost, much still remained, and Oglethorpe's legacy—his brilliant city plan—was still in place.

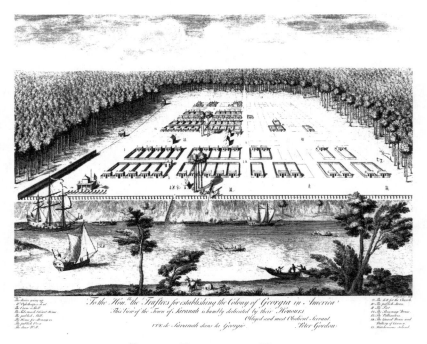

Past—Present—Future

The City Market was the throbbing pulse of downtown in 1953. The vast building teemed with buyers and sellers of everything from fresh fish to okra to peanuts (boiled or parched), and flowers in season.

Could intelligent men and women demolish such a treasure and replace it with a parking garage? That's what happened in 1954, in spite of many objections. The walls came tumbling down, and a colorful slice of life became just a memory. When the City Market was lost and the Davenport House was threatened, sadness turned to fierce resolve in the hearts of the seven women to whom this book is dedicated. They banded together with other concerned Savannahians to form the Historic Savannah Foundation, Inc., a strong organization that began by saving the Davenport House and went on to save many more buildings and areas, demonstrating time and again the economic validity of historic preservation. Since its founding in 1955, Historic Savannah has become a nationwide source of preservation information and inspiration.

Also important in the Savannah saga is the Downtown Neighborhood Association, formed in the 1960s to aid in the effort to preserve Savannah's architectural heritage. Much has been accomplished in the historic district and the adjoining Victorian district, but much remains to be done.

Savannah has been called, "Hostess City of the South," "The Most Beautiful City in North America," and "One of the Top Ten Walking Cities in the United States."

Savannahians treasure these titles and work hard to make them well-deserved. Welcome, and may your stay be enjoyable and memorable.

VISITOR'S CENTER INFORMATION AND TOUR COMPANIES

Visitor Information

• **Savannah Visitor's Center**, 301 Martin Luther King, Jr., Boulevard, (912) 944-0455. Most tours start at the Savannah Visitor's Center, headquarters for information, parking passes, souvenirs, maps, brochures, plenty of free parking, guided bus and trolley tours. Housed in what once was the Central of Georgia Railway Station, the Visitor's Center has a 15-minute orientation slide show every 30 minutes (admission) of Savannah today. Hours: 8:30 a.m.-5 p.m. Mon.-Fri.; 9 a.m.-5 p.m. Sat., Sun., and holidays.

• **Savannah History Museum**, (in the same building as the Savannah Visitor's Center) 303 Martin Luther King, Jr., Boulevard, (912) 238-1779. Here are interesting displays of historical artifacts, plus dramatized history and an 18-minute film of Savannah as Oglethorpe might have seen it. Admission. Open 7 days a week, same hours as Visitor's Center.

• **Savannah International Airport** has an information center in the main terminal, open daily 10 a.m.-6 p.m.

• **Tybee Island Visitor's Center** is open 7 days a week Mar.-Oct., on weekends Nov.-Feb. (912) 786-5444.

Tour Companies

Explore the historic district, Victorian district, forts and islands, house museums, spooky spots and gardens in an air-conditioned bus, in a horse-drawn carriage, or strolling with a guide. For something different, tour the harbor aboard a three-decked riverboat. Reservations recommended.

• **Audio Adventures** — (912) 944-0455. At the Visitor's Center, purchase audio cassettes for walking or driving in and around Savannah. $9.95 each or 2 for $16.95. Video, "We Are Savannah," $12.95.

• **Carriage Tours of Savannah** — (912) 236-6756. Follow the horse's tail and guide's tale down quiet streets and around shady squares. Adults, $9.50; children, $4.50; infants, free.

• **Chatham Area Transit (CAT) Shuttle Bus** — Runs daily with 32 stops in the historic district. Fares: One way, $.50; day pass, $1.50; children under 40 inches tall, free.

• **Classic Tours** — (912) 354-7913. Trolley or bus leaves every 30 minutes from Visitor's Center, or free pick-up in historic district. See the squares, River Street, churches, monuments, neighboring waterfront communities, and more. Adults, $9-$14; ages 4-12, $4-$6; under 4, free. Trolley/River Cruise Combo, $20.

• **Daufuskie Island Water Taxi** — 1-800-398-7687. Round-trip narrated cruise of Intra-coastal Waterway, leaves Tues.-Sat. at 11 a.m. from River Street, returns at 3 p.m. Adults, $15; ages 12 and under, $10. Explore Daufuskie Island in 4-seat golf cart; $29 for 2 hours; guide $5.00.

• **Ghost Walk/Ghost Talk** — (912) 233-3896. A haunted hike to houses with supernatural histories; afternoon departures from Reynolds Square. Adults, $10; ages 5-12, $5.

• **Gray Line Savannah Landmark Tours** — (912) 234-8687. Walking, bus and trolley tours in the historic district, "a living museum," plus nearby Low Country. Adults, $9.50-$20; ages 5-12, $4.50-$8; under age 5, free.

• **Historic Savannah Foundation Convention Consultants** — 1-800-627-5030 or (912) 234-4088. Tours of historic district, Low Country, haunted legends, special interest tours, plus special venues and special meals. Walking or driving tours for 1 person or 3000; $7 to $80; call for schedule and details.

• **Hospitality Tours** — (912) 233-0119. Bus tours around Savannah and out to the forts and islands; pick up at Visitor's Center and all hotels in historic district. Adults, $7-$20; ages 12 and under, $3-$10.

• **Magnolia Carriage Company** — (912) 232-7727. Horse-drawn carriage tours of historic district; departures daily from City Market every hour from 9 a.m.-3 p.m. Adults, $10; ages 4-12, $5; under 4, free.

• **Negro Heritage Trail Tours** — (912) 234-8000. Guided walks or drives to landmarks of African-American history; Mon.-Sat. departures from Visitor's Center at 1 p.m. and 3 p.m. Adults, $10; chidren, $5.

• **Old Savannah Tours** — (912) 354-7913. Departures every 30 minutes from Visitor's Center via bus or trolley; free pick-up in historic district. See squares, house museums, beach, forts, and more. Adults, $9-$14; ages 4-12, $4-$6; under age 4, free. Trolley/River Cruise Combo, $20.

• **Old Town Trolley** — (912) 233-0083. One fare lets you get on and off all day at 7 stops in the historic district; continuous narration. Adults, $14; children, $6.

• **"Queen of Hearts" River Cruises** — (912) 232-9683 or (912) 354-7913. one-hour narrated cruise on Savannah River; departures Tues.-Sun. at 1:30 and 3:30 p.m., plus deejay and pizza Fri. and Sat. at 7, 8, 9, and 10 p.m. Adults, $6; ages 4-12, $3; under age 4, free.

• **"Savannah River Queen" Riverboat Company** — 1-800-786-6404 or (912) 232-6404. Narrated sightseeing of Georgia's port city, departures below City Hall. Sunday brunch, moonlight and dinner cruises, charters. Adults, $8.50-$30.95; age 12 and under, $6-$19.95.

• **Savannah Safari** — (912) 353-9999 or (912) 234-6498. 1–2 hour self-guided walking adventure; hunt terra cotta lion heads, dolphin downspouts, gargoyles; at bookstores and Visitor's Center; author/guide available with 24 hours notice. A delight for all ages.

• **Savannah Tours, Inc.** — (912) 232-3905. Private tailored-for-you tours via van or bus. Departures from Visitor's Center. Adults, $8.50 per hour; $14.50 for 1 1/2 hours; discounts for children.

• **Savannah Trolley Tours** — (912) 234-8687. Narrated trolley tours through the historic district; 250 years of history, homes, and "haints." Adults, $10.50; age 12 and under, $5.

• **Tapestry Tours** – 1-800-794-7770 or (912) 233-7770. Free pick-up. Book all or part of a 6-hour tour of the historic district, plus forts, Tybee, Thunderbolt. Morning 2 hour tour $15; afternoon 4 hour tour, $35; all-day, $50.

• **Tours by B. J.** — 1-800-962-6595 or (912) 233-2335. Morning and evening departures daily from City Market with costumed guides; Ghost Walk leaves from Madison Square on Sun. or by request. $12.50 per person.

• **Tours on Tape** — (912) 944-0455. Rent walking and driving tours on audio tapes; also available in French, German, Spanish, and Italian. One tape, cassette player and map, $8 plus deposit; 2 tapes, $10; 3 tapes, $12. Available at Visitor's Center.

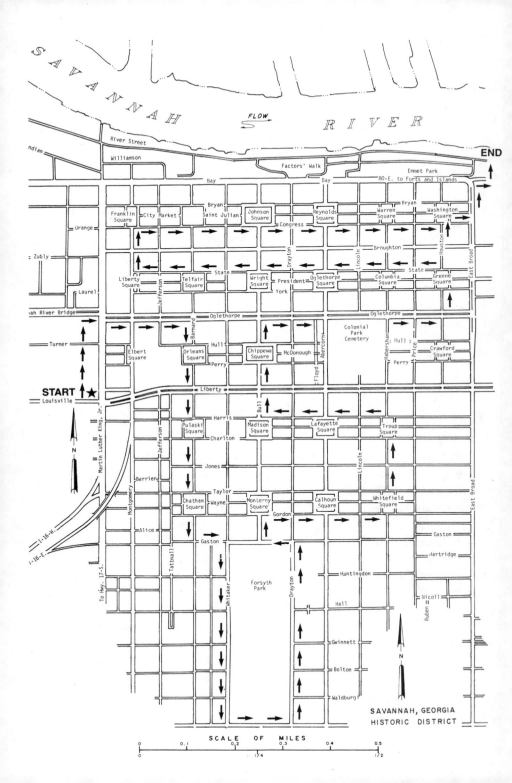

SAVANNAH, GEORGIA
HISTORIC DISTRICT

SAVANNAH PANORAMA
DRIVING TOUR

Savannah Panorama is a **driving tour** of the historic district. The Savannah Visitor's Center is a good starting point. Minimum time required is 1-1 1/2 hours of continuous driving—no stops, no visits to house museums, and no feeding sea gulls or pigeons. We hope your pace will be more leisurely! As this tour is divided into sections, it is easy to make each section into a walking tour if you wish to explore an area more thoroughly.

At each point of interest, we've begun with a block of basic information in **bold-faced type**, followed by supplementary information to read at your leisure.

Drive around each square counterclockwise at least once, and get out and look around if possible.

Remember, Bull Street is like 5th Avenue in New York; it bisects the city from north to south, so streets to the west of Bull Street include West in their name and streets to the east have East in their name. (e.g. West Charlton Street, East Gordon Street).

Because of the amount of foliage in our city, visibility is sometimes obstructed, so look closely for stop signs and street lights.

So, put on your driving hat, keep this book open and handy, and explore Savannah.

Visitor's Center and Savannah History Museum are located at Battlefield Park, the setting in 1779 for the Siege of Savannah, a bloody battle of the American Revolution in which the patriots tried (unsuccessfully) to wrench Savannah from the British. For over 100 years beginning in 1833, the area was headquarters for the Central of Georgia Railway Company. Much can still be seen of this significant antebellum railroad complex. For visiting hours and fees, see Museums, Historic Houses and Forts.

The Visitor's Center was the Central of Georgia passenger depot. Also nearby are the roundhouse and repair shops, even Baldwin 103, an original Central of Georgia locomotive. The museum offers a film covering Savannah's history from 1733 to the present.

This poignant place, so steeped in Savannah history, is a good place to begin Savannah Panorama.

DIRECTIONS: Follow exit arrows out of Visitor's Center; cross Turner Street; turn right onto Oglethorpe Avenue; go through 2 traffic lights and across Jefferson Street and turn right onto Barnard Street.

Orleans Square

This square was named for the 1815 victory of General Andrew "Old Hickory" Jackson in the Battle of New Orleans, during the War of 1812. The fountain was given in 1989 by Savannah's German heritage organizations, one of the many groups included and treasured in Savannah's ethnic diversity. Orleans Square was added to the city plan in 1815.

Points of interest:
1. Savannah Civic Center
2. Champion-McAlpin-Fowlkes House
3. 114 and 116 West Hull Street

• **Savannah Civic Center** (1971), west side of square.
Center for everything from symphony concerts to tractor pulls.
    The Civic Center was built on the site of the Bulloch-

Habersham House, designed by William Jay (c. 1820) and razed by the city of Savannah in 1914, before historic preservation had become a priority.

• **Champion-McAlpin-Fowlkes House** (1842), 230 Barnard Street.
Two-story Corinthian columns on a masterpiece of Greek Revival architecture.
Irish architect Charles Blaney Cluskey is credited with the design for this mansion of scored stucco over brick. Note the graceful curves of the sandstone entrance stairs. First to own and occupy the house was bank president, Aaron Champion. During the Civil War, Champion hid his bank's gold in a well at the rear of the garden. After the war, he went to the well and recovered all but one ten dollar gold piece! Champion bequeathed his house to his only daughter, Maria Sophia, who had become Mrs. James W. McAlpin. She also inherited Hermitage Plantation from her father. (That's the plantation where Henry McAlpin manufactured Savannah grey bricks and whose foundry was first to produce cast iron in Savannah.) In 1939, Miss Alida Harper (later Mrs. Hunter McGuire Fowlkes) acquired the house she had loved for years. Today the house belongs to the Georgia Chapter, Society of the Cincinnati.

• **114 and 116 West Hull Street** (1817), at corner of West Hull and Barnard, next to the parking lot.
A pair of houses with high "stoops" (from Dutch "stoep," for veranda or porch.)
With tin roofs and twin dormers, these houses were designed in 1817 by John Ash, builder. For many years, until his death in 1974, No. 116 was home to historian Walter Charlton Hartridge and his family. "Big Walter" was handsome, courtly, energetic, and articulate. How he loved to stride through the streets of his beloved city, gathering historical data for his scholarly books and articles.

DIRECTIONS: Continue around square and go south on Barnard Street to Pulaski Square. Remember—Oaks are beautiful, but they obscure vision, so proceed carefully.

Pulaski Square

Named for Polish Count Casimir Pulaski, hero of the Revolutionary War, this square is shaded by nineteen majestic oak trees and was laid out in 1837. Idealistic young Count Pulaski fought on the side of the patriots in the War for American Independence. On October 12, 1779, he was knocked from his horse by a bullet during the Siege of Savannah. He died a few hours later. A monument to Count Pulaski stands in Monterey Square on Bull Street. He was also honored in the naming of Fort Pulaski, a "must see" on the Forts and Islands Tour.

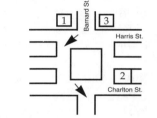

Points of interest:
1. Margaret Murphy House
2. Pulaski House
3. Francis Stebbins Bartow House

• **Margaret Murphy House** (1992), 200 West Harris Street. **Handsome blue corner building; compatible, new construction in the historic district.**
    Constructed in Savannah's favorite "high stoop" design, this house was named for Margaret Murphy Green, longtime friend to the neighborhood and assistant to the antiques dealer whose shop once stood on this corner.

• **Pulaski House** (1915), 328 Barnard Street. **Massive red brick structure with green awnings—a dormitory for the Savannah College of Art and Design (SCAD).** Once housed the Jewish Educational Alliance and the Salvation Army.

• **Francis Stebbins Bartow House** (c. 1850) 128 West Harris Street, at Barnard.
Corner clapboard house with side porches.

This house was built for the family of Civil War hero Francis Stebbins Bartow, who died in 1861 in the first Battle of Bull Run, after leading Savannah's Oglethorpe Light Infantry to Richmond. His grave is in Laurel Grove Cemetery. The rank of brigadier general was awarded posthumously. Busts of General Bartow and General Lafayette McLaws, also a Confederate hero, flank the Confederate Monument in Forsyth Park.

DIRECTIONS: Continue around square and south on Barnard Street to Chatham Square.

Chatham Square

Chatham Square honors William Pitt, Earl of Chatham. As Savannah grew southward, Chatham Square was added in 1847. Its namesake was a stalwart ally of the colonists in the English Parliament.

Points of interest:
1. **Barnard Hall**
2. **Gordon Row**

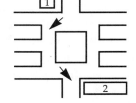

• **Barnard Hall**, 212 West Taylor Street.
SCAD classroom building in yellow with turquoise trim.
    Liberal Arts students of Savannah College of Art and Design come here for art history or architecture classes, or to use the slide library. Spiffily painted and topped with Ludowici tile, it is one of the many formerly abandoned school buildings which SCAD now utilizes.

• **Gordon Row** (1854), West Gordon Street, beginning at Barnard.
15 almost-identical brick houses.
    Each house in this row has three stories on a high basement and a back yard. In the 1950s, one could be purchased for $1,500.00.

DIRECTIONS: Continue around square and south on Barnard Street for one more block; turn left onto Gaston Street for one block to traffic light; turn right at Whitaker Street and look right to see:

• **Georgia Historical Society (Hodgson Hall)** (1875), 501 Whitaker Street. (912) 651-2128.
A library specializing in historic records and research.
Overlooking Forsyth Park, Hodgson Hall was built by sisters Mary Telfair and Margaret Telfair Hodgson as a memorial to Margaret's husband, William Brown Hodgson, and as a home for one of his scholarly interests, the venerable Georgia Historical Society, organized in 1839. Architect Detlef Lienau used stucco-over-brick construction. Well-known both as scholar and Middle East diplomat, Hodgson was acquainted with 14 languages and spoke 9 fluently. His favorite was Berber, language of the Sahara desert, into which he translated the Gospel of Matthew. A splendid portrait of Hodgson hangs in the main reading room, as does the panorama of Savannah in 1837 by Fermin Cerveau. GHS hours are 10 a.m.-6 p.m. Tues.-Fri. and 9 a.m.-3 p.m. on Sat. No charge, and staff members are friendly and helpful.

DIRECTIONS: Take left lane; circle Forsyth Park.

Forsyth Park

26 acres for bench sitting, walking, jogging, tennis, Ultimate Frisbee, soccer, football, pigeon feeding.
Brainchild of William Brown Hodgson, Forsyth Park dates from 1851. The name honors John Forsyth, American statesman and governor of Georgia in 1828. Planting was outlined by Bavarian landscape architect

Wilhelm Christian Bischoff.

Under that halo of mist in the middle of the park is a white, cast-iron fountain with spouting tritons, similar to the fountain in Place de la Concorde, Paris, and the twin of one in Cuzco, Peru.

In the middle, beyond the fountain, is the Monument to Confederate Dead in the Civil War. Gift of G. W. J. DeRenne, this monument by British sculptor David Richards was installed in 1879. It bears these poignant words, "Come from the four winds, O Breath, and breathe upon these slain that they may live."

At the southern end of the park at Park Avenue stands the bronze soldier commemorating Georgians who died in the Spanish-American War.

At the Gaston Street end of the park is the Monument to the United States Marine Corps, dedicated in 1949.

DIRECTIONS: Turn left onto Gaston Street; go one block and turn right onto Bull Street. Pull over to see:

• **George Ferguson Armstrong House (1920)**, 447 Bull Street, first house on the left.
White brick mansion, built for shipping executive who served in Spanish-American War.

George Armstrong served with the Chatham Artillery in the Spanish-American War. He built this house in 1920 (Henrik Wallin, architect) of brick with a snowy glaze. The design is Ecole des Beaux Arts, reminiscent of buildings of this period in Paris. Armstrong State College, now south of the city, began here in 1935 as Armstrong Junior College, thanks to Mrs. Armstrong's bequest of the house for education. Now it's home to a law firm.

• **Oglethorpe Club** (1857), 450 Bull Street, on the right.
Private club, established in 1870.
   This stately brick house on the corner of Bull and Gaston was built for British consul Edmund Molyneux. Later it was owned by Civil War General Henry Rootes Jackson.

DIRECTIONS: Continue north on Bull Street to Monterey Square.

Monterey Square

Monterey Square commemorates the capture of Monterey, Mexico, by General Zachary Taylor in 1846. Here stands the monument to that gallant Polish officer, Casimir Pulaski. The sculptor was Robert E. Launitz. (Yes, the Pulaski statue is not in Pulaski Square.) We recommend at least two complete circuits of this beautiful square, laid out in 1847.

Points of interest:
1. **Congregation Mickve Israel**
2. **Thomas Levy House**
3. **William Hunter House**
4. **Hugh M. Comer House**
5. **10 West Taylor Street**
6. **423 and 425 Bull Street**
7. **Mercer House**
8. **Noble Hardee House**
9. **Scudders' Range**

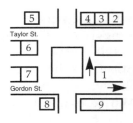

• **Congregation Mickve Israel**, Bull Street on Monterey Square.
Historic synagogue with Gothic architecture.
   Let's pause to admire the sanctuary of one the oldest Jewish congregations in the south, and the third oldest in the nation. Its first members included the Sephardic and Ashkenazic Jewish settlers who came to Georgia aboard the *William and Sarah* arriving just a few months after Oglethorpe. Congregation Mickve Israel received a perpetual charter from Governor Edward

Telfair in 1790. Gothic in design (unusual for a synagogue), this building was consecrated in 1878. Of special interest in the synagogue's museum is the 15th century Torah brought over by the early settlers.

• **Thomas Levy House** (1867; 1896), 12 East Taylor Street, to the right.
Exuberantly baroque residence and print shop with Georgia marble steps, curved windows above the main entrance.
Built in 1867, this house was remodeled in 1896 in the Second Empire Baroque style. The house was featured in the 1979 movie, *Orphan Train*. The basement now houses a fine antique map, book, and print shop.

• **William Hunter House** (c. 1872), 10 East Taylor Street.
Side galleries on two stories, golden yellow stucco.
Cast iron, exterior "eyebrows" accent the windows of this newly-restored, 4-story house.

• **Hugh M. Comer House** (1880), 2 East Taylor Street.
Corner house with a pair of palm trees in front, "bed and breakfast" below.
Italianate in design (arched windows, burnt sienna stucco), this stucco-over-brick dwelling was built for Hugh M. Comer, president of the Central of Georgia Railway Company. Jefferson Davis and his daughter, Winnie, visited the Comers in 1886.

• **10 West Taylor Street** (1852).
Sunset pink stucco with cast iron entrance stairs.
The original 2-story brick house was augmented in the early 1900s with cast iron balconies, Ludowici tile roof, and Dutch Colonial third floor. The result is a mid-19th-century house with a New Orleans accent. (When Emmeline was growing up here, she built up her biceps

by hauling her younger sister up and down in the "dumb wait-
er" that once carried hot hominy to the dining room from the
basement kitchen. In true southern tradition, their pediatrician
father came in from the office wing each day for 2 o'clock dinner.)

• **423 and 425 Bull Street** (1858).
Exquisite ironwork, reminiscent of Gramercy Park.
    This pre-Civil War pair of houses was built of scored stucco
over brick. First owner was a Presbyterian minister, Dr. Charles
W. Rogers. Unusual details are cast iron porticoes and covered
balconies. The office at 427 Bull Street (below 425) is used by
Leopold Adler II, recipient of the National Trust for Historic
Preservation's highest honor, the Crowninshield Award.

• **Mercer House** (1860-71), 429 Bull Street.
Red brick, framed by handsome iron fence.
    This Italianate house was designed by architect John S.
Norris for General Hugh Weedon Mercer prior to the Civil War,
but was not completed until the war was over. With gracefully
arched doors and windows opening onto cast iron balconies, it
stands on a trust lot. Proudly it stands, but cannot speak of the
tragic last years of a well-known antiques dealer who restored
the house in the 1960s and 1970s and lived here until his death. A
descendant of General Mercer was well-known lyricist Johnny
Mercer.

• **Noble Hardee House** (1860-69), 3 West Gordon Street and 441
Bull Street.
**Residence and antiques shop at corner of Bull and Gordon;
wrap-around cast iron balcony.**
    Noble Hardee began this mansion in 1860, but died before the
house was finally completed after the Civil War. President
Chester A. Arthur, who visited here twice during his presiden-
cy, no doubt enjoyed the view of Monterey Square. The original
design of the house is gradually being restored as later additions are removed. It was part of Armstrong Junior College in
the 1940s.

• **Scudders' Range** (c.1852), l-9 East Gordon Street.
Outstanding row of town houses, overlooking Monterey Square.
These were built by brothers John and Ephraim Scudder. Construction is of stucco over Savannah grey brick, with ornamental iron balconies. The buildings exemplify merchant town housing that is characteristic of the mid-19th century.

DIRECTIONS: Continue east on East Gordon Street to Calhoun Square.

Calhoun Square

Named for one of the south's great statesmen, this southernmost square on Abercorn Street was added in 1851. John Caldwell Calhoun served his country in many capacities, including Vice-President, Secretary of State, and Secretary of War. Each year, school children from all over the city gather here to "dance the Maypole" in front of Massie Heritage Center, a tradition that began in the 1850s.

Points of interest:
1. Massie Heritage Interpretation Center
2. 430-432 Abercorn Street
3. 202 East Taylor Street
4. Wesley Monumental United Methodist Church

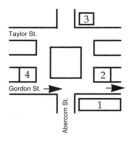

• **Massie Heritage Interpretation Center** (c. 1855-56), 201-213 East Gordon Street.
Rosy-beige school buildings with connecting walkways, named for Peter Massie, Scottish planter who came to Georgia.
Thanks to a bequest from Peter Massie, who lived south of Savannah, plans were drawn by architect John S. Norris for a school which opened in 1856 to educate Savannah's less fortu-

nate children. These buildings, closed for regular classes since 1974, are part of Georgia's oldest chartered public school. Still owned and operated by the Savannah-Chatham County Public Schools, Massie is now a resource center in living history, offering permanent exhibits of Savannah's City Plan, Savannah in the Victorian Era, and Elements of Greek, Roman, and Gothic Architecture. School children come here to learn about local history and architecture, and to experience a 19th century school day. Hours are Mon.-Fri., 9 a.m.-4 p.m. No charge, but donations are welcome.

• **430-432 Abercorn Street** (c. 1855).
Brick residence with decorative ironwork, bay window above entrance.
Here's a mid-19th century dwelling on a trust lot with a jewel of a carriage house behind.

• **202 East Taylor Street** (mid-19th century).
Side garden with view through cast iron gate; flower beds outlined with up-ended ale bottles from brewery of first owner, William Rogers.
On the northeast corner of Taylor and Abercorn stands a recently restored and renovated mid-19th century brick residence with 3 stories on a basement. A former owner had fun recovering lost details, such as tracking an unexplained chimney to a plastered-over fireplace in an upstairs bathroom.

• **Wesley Monumental United Methodist Church**, Abercorn Street on Calhoun Square.
Soaring spires and Gothic arches on a church named for English clergy brothers John and Charles Wesley, founders of Methodism.
Begun in 1868, the church was not dedicated until 1890, because of Reconstruction money woes and a yellow fever epidemic. The sanctuary of this busy parish seats 1000; a new Noack organ was dedicated in 1985. "Methodism with a warm heart" is the motto here.

DIRECTIONS: Continue two blocks east on Gordon Street (cross Lincoln Street) to Whitefield Square.

Whitefield Square

This square was named for the spirited English clergyman who was minister to the colonists, then founded Bethesda Orphan Home. Practice pronouncing Whitefield to rhyme with Pittfield, in honor of the Rev. George Whitefield, who in 1738 succeeded the Rev. John Wesley as Church of England minister to the Georgia colony. He is also remembered as founder (in 1740) of Bethesda Home for Boys, America's oldest orphanage in continuous operation. The gazebo in the center of Whitefield Square is a favorite spot for exchanging "I do's." Frame houses with wide porches and Victorian "gingerbread" abound in this neighborhood.

DIRECTIONS: Go around square to see:

• **First Congregational Church**, United Church of Christ, Habersham Street on Whitefield Square.
White Gothic church building with tin roof.
   First Congregational Church is an outgrowth of the Alfred E. Beach Institute, originally a school where white missionary teachers taught African-American children. Organized in 1869, shortly after the Civil War, the congregation acquired this property in 1878. This Gothic building replaces the original, frame meeting house.

DIRECTIONS: Circle square and exit with right turn at Red Cross Building onto Habersham Street; go two blocks to Troup Square.

Troup Square

The astronomical centerpiece and the square are named for Georgia governor (1823-27) George Michael Troup. In the center, poised on six turtles, is an armillary sphere, an "astronomical model with solid rings, all circles of a single sphere, used to display relationships among the principal celestial circles." Whew! Laid out in 1851, this square commemorates Governor Troup, who welcomed the Marquis de Lafayette to Savannah in 1825, and later served as United States senator. A unique water fountain for animals has two low-slung bowls for lapping, plus a filling mechanism.

• **Savannah Baptist Center**, Habersham Street on Troup Square. **Why is this Gothic church called the "Jingle Bells Church"?**
   Savannah Baptist Center (once a Unitarian church) is known as the "Jingle Bells Church" because in 1850, James L. Pierpont, who was serving here as organist and music director, composed this beloved Christmas song.

DIRECTIONS: Continue west on Harris Street to Lafayette Square.

Lafayette Square

The name of this square honors the Marquis de Lafayette, whose full name was Marie Joseph Paul Yves Roch Gilbert de Motier. Aide to George Washington in the War for American Independence, the Marquis visited Savannah in 1825 and spoke to cheering Savannahians (see R. Owens-Thomas House). Lafayette Square dates from 1837. The fountain was given by the Savannah Town Committee of The National Society of The Colonial Dames of America in the State of Georgia. Colonial Dames headquarters, overlooking Lafayette Square, is the Andrew Low House Museum, described below.

Points of interest:
1. **Cathedral of Saint John the Baptist**
2. **Andrew Low House Museum**
3. **Battersby-Hartridge-Anderson House**
4. **Flannery O'Connor Childhood Home**
5. **Hamilton-Turner House**

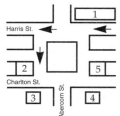

• **Cathedral of Saint John the Baptist**, Abercorn Street at Lafayette Square.
Oldest Roman Catholic church in Georgia, across Lincoln Street, on the right.

Twin spires with chiming bells rise high above this French Gothic cathedral, seat of the Diocese of Savannah. Dedicated in 1876, it was destroyed by fire in 1898, then rebuilt from the original plans of Francis Baldwin, architect. The interior is rich with Italian marble, Austrian stained glass, and opulent Persian rugs. The first event of St. Patrick's Day on March 17 each year is Mass in the cathedral; then the Hibernians head for Forsyth Park to march in a parade that's second only to New York City's. Savannah (even the water in the fountains) is green for a day!

• **Andrew Low House Museum**, 329 Abercorn Street, (912) 233-6854.
Headquarters of The National Society of The Colonial Dames of America in the State of Georgia.

Andrew Low and his wife, Sarah Hunter Low, began this house in 1847 with the help of architect John S. Norris. Their plan to live here with their 3 children was wrecked first by the death of 4-year-old Andrew, then Sarah Low herself died a few months later. After years of loneliness, Andrew was married to Mary Couper Stiles, who bore him 4 daughters and one son, William Mackay Low. William was called "Billow" by Juliette Magill "Daisy" Gordon, to whom he was married at Christ Church in 1886. They lived in and traveled from this imposing stucco-over-brick mansion. The marriage of Daisy and Billow was unhappy, childless, and soon they parted. Daisy Low had daughters aplenty, though, when she founded the Girl Scouts of The United States of America in 1912. Andrew Low House was visited by William Makepeace Thackeray and General Robert Edward Lee. It's a "must see" house museum that's open daily (except Thursdays and major holidays) from 10:30 a.m. until 4:30 p.m. Admission.

• **Battersby-Hartridge-Anderson House** (1852), 119 East Charlton Street.
A brick residence in a design that's typical in Charleston, rare in Savannah.
William Battersby built this brick house in 1852 on land purchased from friend and neighbor, Andrew Low. The front door opens onto a two-story side porch, or veranda. (In Charleston, they call them "piazzas.") The original garden plan has been preserved in the walled "parterre" garden. ("Parterre" means that paths, beds, and hedges form a pattern.)

• **Flannery O'Connor Childhood Home** (c. 1855), 207 East Charlton Street. (912) 233-6014.
High-stooped house museum with schedule of lectures and readings.
This 3-story house once was home to Edward and Regina O'Connor, whose only child, Mary Flannery, dropped the Mary in college and became famous as one of this country's outstanding authors. Flannery at age 6 was seen in a national newscast with her pet chicken, which she had trained to walk backward. She died in 1964 of lupus erythematosus, the same disease that had claimed her father in 1941. Her childhood home is now a house museum where readings of her work are presented regularly.

• **Hamilton-Turner House** (1873), 330 Abercorn Street.
Outstanding example of Second Empire architecture with four iron balconies; house museum and gift shop.
Commissioned by Samuel P. Hamilton, this privately-owned

house museum was constructed by Abraham Snedeker, builder. Exterior brick was later covered with stucco. Pause to revel in the elaborate Victorian ornamentation, from mansard roof on down. Guided tours are offered daily, 10 a.m. until 4 p.m. Admission.

DIRECTIONS: Exit square on Harris Street; cross Drayton Street, heading for two blocks to Madison Square.

Madison Square

This square was named for fourth United States president, James Madison. Atop the monument stands Sergeant William Jasper, Revolutionary War hero, holding aloft the banner he has just recaptured for his company. Unveiled in 1888, the monument is the work of sculptor Alexander Doyle. Around the base are scenes from this gallant soldier's life. In one, we see him wounded and dying, cradled in the arms of a comrade. Colonial roadways are marked by cannons on the south side of the square, including the old route to Darien, Georgia mapped out in 1733 with the help of Chief Tomochichi. Madison Square was added in 1837. General William Tecumseh Sherman was headquartered across from this square at the Green-Meldrim House in 1864.

Points of interest:
1. Sorrel-Weed House
2. St. John's Episcopal Church Parish House/Green-Meldrim House Museum
3. St. John's Episcopal Church
4. Savannah College of Art and Design
5. Eliza Jewett House
6. DeSoto-Hilton

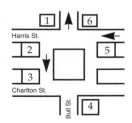

• **Sorrel-Weed House** (c. 1841), 6 West Harris Street.
Stuccoed building with welcoming-arms stairs at entrance.
    Charles Blaney Cluskey, Irish architect, designed this elegant dwelling for the Sorrel family. Cluskey's love of Greek Revival design is seen in accents of Doric columns, a sweeping double entrance and marble floors. In deference to torrid Savannah summers, Cluskey drew plans for the main floor so that all rooms open onto a shaded veranda. One distinguished member of the Sorrel family was Gilbert Moxley Sorrel, known as Moxley. Young Moxley was a bank clerk in Savannah when the Civil War began. He fought with the Confederates, served as one of Lee's lieutenants, was wounded three times and, by age 26, held the rank of brigadier general. Later, the house was owned by the Weed family. Now it is a private residence with shop attached. Two other Cluskey buildings face each other in this block at 14 and 18 West Harris.

ST. JOHN'S CHURCH, SAVANNAH, GEORGIA.

• **St. John's Episcopal Church Parish House** (1863), 14 West Macon Street, also known as the **Green-Meldrim House Museum.** (912) 233-3845. **Medieval styled architecture with unusual oriel windows.** From crenellated parapet to metal-studded portal, the design is Gothic and the mood medieval. First owner was cotton merchant, Charles Green; John S. Norris was builder-architect. Union General William Tecumseh Sherman had headquarters here when Savannah surrendered to him toward the end of the Civil War. Serving then as mayor pro-tem of Savannah was Polly's great-great-grandfather, City Alderman George Washington Wylly. Sherman sent the following telegram to President Abraham Lincoln in December, 1864: "I beg to present you as a Christmas gift the city of Savannah..." A later owner was Judge Peter Meldrim, mayor of Savannah, and father of beautiful daughters. Toward the end of her long life, Sophie Meldrim Shonnard was still beautiful as she adjusted her pink boa in her apartment on Perry Street, asking just the right questions to make each guest feel special. The house became a National Historic Landmark in 1976. Visiting hours are 10 a.m.-4 p.m. on Tues., Thurs., Fri., and Sat. Donations.

• **St. John's Episcopal Church**, Bull Street on Madison Square. **Gothic church with connecting garden to parish house.**
Gothic in design and dating from the mid-1850s, St. John's was designed by Calvin Otis. Dark wood and rich colors contribute to an atmosphere of quiet beauty. The sound of St. John's carillon has long been a melodious gift to the neighborhood. Between church and parish house, Macon Street was closed to traffic to make room for a gracious garden.

• **Savannah College of Art and Design (SCAD)**, 342 Bull Street. (912) 238-2400.
Romanesque red brick with up-ended cannon flanking entrance, built to be Savannah Volunteer Guards Armory.
Just a bit south of Madison Square, on Bull Street, is the first building SCAD acquired, designed in 1893 by William Gibbons Preston. Combined here are red brick and beautifully molded terra cotta, a favorite combination in this period. Since its beginning in 1979, SCAD has renovated and utilized many downtown buildings. The growth of the college has brought vitality into many downtown neighborhoods. Gallery A, at the corner, offers students' work for view or purchase.

• **Eliza Jewett House** (1843), 326 Bull Street, on Madison Square.
Classical residence with bookstore on street level.
Prosperous realtor, Eliza Jewett, built this house of stucco over brick. It is doubly blessed by the expanse of Madison Square in front and Shaver's Bookstore below. In the 1950s, monocled character actor Charles Coburn came here often to

visit his sister, Zoe.

• **DeSoto-Hilton Hotel**, 15 East Liberty Street, (912) 232-9000.
Modern hotel-bank complex in intriguing shopping area.
   Local crafts, antiques, gifts, clothing, restaurants, books, old
and new—all are within easy reach.

DIRECTIONS: Exit square with right turn onto Bull Street;
cross Liberty Street and head north to Chippewa Square.

Chippewa Square

Chippewa Square was named to commemorate the victory of
American troops under General Jacob Brown in the Battle of
Chippewa, War of 1812. In the center is a handsome bronze
sculpture by Daniel Chester French of James Edward
Oglethorpe in the full dress uniform of a British general. His
right hand rests on his unsheathed sword; his eyes gaze southward toward Florida, ever guarding Georgia from the threat of
the Spaniards. (Yes, the Oglethorpe statue is not in Oglethorpe
Square.) Henry Bacon, who designed the base of the monument, also teamed with Daniel French to create the Lincoln
Memorial in Washington, D. C.

Points of interest:
1. Savannah Theatre
2. First Baptist Church

Hull St.

2   1

Perry St.

Bull St.

• **Savannah Theatre**, 222 Bull Street.
**Live theater in an art deco building on the country's oldest
theater site in continuous operation; a Greek Revival building
by William Jay once stood here.**
   First on this site was the 1000-seat theater designed in 1818
by the English architect, William Jay, and built by Amos
Scudder of New Jersey. It took Mr. Scudder three months to
transport his carpentry tools to Savannah by oxcart! It's said
that patrons of the first production, *The Soldier's Daughter*, paid

$1.00 for a box seat and 50 cents for a perch in the gallery. Used both for opera and drama, the stage of this theater hosted such stars as Edwin Booth, Sarah Bernhardt, Lillian Russell, and Savannah's own Charles Coburn. Conversion for films and a succession of fires consumed most of the original building, even its collection of programs and memorabilia. Today's visitor sees 1950s architecture, now home to the Savannah Theatre Company, a community enterprise offering a season of live drama, plus a summer musical. (912) 233-7764

• **First Baptist Church** (1833), Bull Street on Chippewa Square. **Church in Greek temple design with six massive columns.**
    This is a missionary Baptist congregation with the motto, "Established in Faith; Nurtured in Hope; Continuing in Love." A Savannah city ordinance of 1791 established a Baptist society at Houston and Duke (now Congress) Streets. The first minister was Dr. Henry Holcombe, who organized The First Baptist Church in Savannah in 1800. There's a strong music program here and an organ built by Ernest M. Skinner.

DIRECTIONS: Continue around square and turn right on Bull Street to Oglethorpe Avenue. Just before Oglethorpe Avenue, pull aside and look right to see:

• **Savannah-Chatham County Public Schools, Administrative Offices**, 208 Bull Street (Formerly Chatham Academy and Savannah High School.)
The entrance to Chatham Academy was on Oglethorpe Avenue near Drayton Street; one entered Savannah High School via the broad stairs on Bull Street; today these buildings house the offices of Savannah public schools.
    Organized in 1788, Chatham Academy moved in 1908 to the building designed by Henry Urban, architect, on Oglethorpe Avenue. For a time, Chatham Academy was Savannah's only public high school. Then the building around the corner at 208 Bull Street became Savannah High School from 1925 until 1937. Today the buildings are home to the administrative offices of the Savannah-Chatham Board of Public Education.

• **Independent Presbyterian Church**, at Bull and Oglethorpe, on the left.
A soaring steeple with clocks on all four sides, topped by a gleaming, brass weathervane.
Organized in 1755, this congregation has strong Scottish ties. A colorful event each year is the Kirkin' o' the Tartans, (when bagpipes skir-r-rl and kilts twir-r-r-r-l, all on a Sunday mor-r-r-r-nin'). In 1818, architect John Holden Greene won a design competition with his plans for this magnificent building. When the church burned in 1889, architect William Gibbons Preston directed the rebuilding to the original plans. (Emmeline was glad to have her father's arm to support her when she walked down the long, center aisle in 1955 to marry her Robert Scotland Cooper.)

DIRECTIONS: Look across Oglethorpe Avenue to the northeast corner building to see:

• **Juliette Gordon Low Girl Scout National Center (Wayne-Gordon House Museum c. 1818),** across Oglethorpe Avenue on the right, facing south. (912) 233-4501. **An imposing Regency mansion in shades of brown, birthplace of Juliette Gordon Low, who founded the Girl Scouts of the United States of America in 1912.**
Juliette Gordon Low was born here on Halloween night in 1860. Did English architect, William Jay, design this mansion? Some say "yes," some say "no." At any rate, this elegant town house was built for James Moore Wayne, mayor of Savannah and Supreme Court Justice, who sold it to Juliette's grandfather, William Washington Gordon, in 1831. The furnishings reflect the years of Juliette's girlhood, including her portrait and many

family furnishings. House and gift shop are open six days a week. Admission.

DIRECTIONS: Turn right and head east on Oglethorpe Avenue; to your left is:

• **Colonial Park Cemetery**. Gates given by the Daughters of the American Revolution (DAR).
Cemetery used for 100 years, beginning in 1750.
   In 1777, a famous duel was fought between Lachlan McIntosh and Declaration of Independence signer Button Gwinnett. Gwinnett was mortally wounded and died a few days later. Opponents in life, they're neighbors in death in Colonial Park Cemetery. The Trustees' Garden Club has done much to maintain and restore the cemetery by installing lighting, repairing broken sidewalks, as well as pruning and planting.

DIRECTIONS: On your right is:

• **Mary Marshall Row** (1855), East Oglethorpe Avenue, facing south, ending at Lincoln Street.
Four houses that were within hours of being demolished in 1960 for their valuable Savannah grey bricks and marble steps.
   The carriage houses had already been leveled when Polly Tucker (Mrs. F. Bland Tucker) brought the news that someone was about to start wrecking the four exceptional brick houses built by Mary Magdalene Leaver Marshall. Four pioneer preservationists—Albert Stoddard, Lee Adler, Karl Roebling, and Harry Duncan—moved quickly to buy all four houses, thus realizing one of the early victories of Historic Savannah Foundation, Inc. One of the houses was occupied by Pulitzer prize-winning poet and author Conrad Aiken and his wife Mary when they returned to Savannah in 1962.

DIRECTIONS: Continue on Oglethorpe Avenue to Houston Street; turn left on Houston Street to Greene Square.

Greene Square

This square was named for General Nathanael Greene, aide to George Washington in the Revolutionary War. General Greene was also honored by the obelisk in Johnson Square, where he and his son are now buried. In gratitude for his service, General Greene was given Mulberry Grove Plantation, where he died at 44 of sunstroke. It was at Mulberry Grove in 1793 that young Eli Whitney took time out from tutoring the four Greene children to invent the cotton gin, with the help of Catherine Littlefield "Caty" Greene, widow of the brave General.

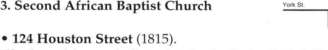

Points of interest:
1. 124 Houston Street
2. 536 East State Street
3. Second African Baptist Church

• **124 Houston Street** (1815).
Clapboard house believed to be built for Isaiah Davenport, a builder himself, who came to Savannah from Rhode Island.

• **536 East State Street** (1845).
A red frame house, built for John Dorsett.
This tiny treasure was moved to its present location by preservation pioneer, Stella Henderson, who also restored the house at 131 Houston Street.

• **Second African Baptist Church**, Houston Street on Greene Square.
Sherman and Stanton met here with newly-freed slaves just after the end of the Civil War.
The Reverend Henry Cunningham founded this congregation just after Christmas in 1802. Visitors after the Civil War were Union General William Tecumseh Sherman and Edwin McMaster Stanton, U. S. Secretary of War. In 1925, the pulpit was rescued from a devastating fire.

DIRECTIONS: Continue west on State Street; to your right are:

• **Anderson Row** (c. 1870), 502-512 East State Street.

• **Timothy Bonticou House** (c.1815), 418 East State Street. **Double wooden house with blue trim; moved from Broughton Street.**

• **416 East State Street** (late 1700s).
Frame house set back from street; garden in front.
This small, wooden Davenport-designed house is known as Laura's House. It was moved from another location and once was home to a tea room that had the best Sally Lunn bread in town!

DIRECTIONS: Continue on State Street to Columbia Square.

Columbia Square

Remember singing "Columbia, the Gem of the Ocean" ? Then you already know that Columbia is a female personification for the good old USA! Ferns and flowers adorn the fountain given in 1970 by Eudora and Wainwright Roebling in memory of her parents, Augusta and Wymberley DeRenne. The fountain came from Wormsloe, home of Noble Jones who came over with Oglethorpe. Columbia Square and Greene Square were added to the original town plan in 1799.

Points of interest:
1. Francis Stone House
2. Isaiah Davenport House Museum
3. The Kehoe House

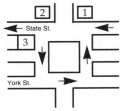

• **Francis Stone House** (1821), 402-404 East State Street.
High-stooped, white, frame house with black trim; built for city alderman Francis Stone. Francis Stone, who built this house, was given "five shares of Central Railroad" in gratitude

for his service during the yellow fever epidemic of 1854.

• **Isaiah Davenport House Museum** (1815-21), 324 East State Street. (912) 233-8097. **First house saved by the seven women to whom this book is dedicated.** Here's the linch-pin of historic preservation in Savannah. It was the threat of destruction of this house that prompted seven strong Savannah women in 1955 to band together in outraged opposition. This band of seven grew into the vital organization now known as the Historic Savannah Foundation, Inc. History tells that builder Isaiah Davenport came from Rhode Island and married Sarah Rosamund Clark. In 1818, Davenport became a city alderman and began construction of this distinguished residence. Built of brick in Federal style, Davenport House is rich with delicate wrought iron. The sweeping, double entrance has a fanlight over the front door. Now a house museum with garden and gift shop, Davenport House is furnished to reflect the life style of Isaiah and Sarah, its first occupants. Hours are 10 a.m.-4 p.m. daily except Thurs. and from 1-4 p.m. on Sun. It's owned by Historic Savannah, and income is used to fund HSF projects. Admission.

• **The Kehoe House, Consul Court** (c. 1890), 123 Habersham Street. (912) 232-1020.
Red brick and terra cotta, built for William J. Kehoe, founder of Kehoe Iron Works. DeWitt Bruyn, architect.
Mr. Kehoe, an Irishman, was the father of nine children. When the eldest daughter and her five children came home to live, Mr. Kehoe often packed up rosary and newspaper and climbed to the cupola (long since rotted away) for respite. The mood of the house is Romantic Revival, and there's handcarved

oak woodwork inside, plus twelve marble mantels. Long a haven to the weary, Kehoe House was once a funeral home and is now an inn.

DIRECTIONS: Exit square on State Street, headed west (cross Lincoln Street) to Oglethorpe Square.

Oglethorpe Square

This square was laid out in 1742 and named for James Edward Oglethorpe, founder of the Georgia colony. No central monument here, but there is a memorial to the pacifist Moravians who arrived in 1736 on the same ship that brought John and Charles Wesley to Savannah. (The Oglethorpe monument is in Chippewa Square.)

Points of interest:
1. Cluskey Buildings
2. (Richardson)-Owens-Thomas House Museum and Regency Shop

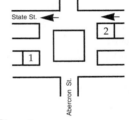

• **Cluskey Buildings** (1830), 127 Abercorn Street.
Brick office buildings with leafy ironwork, blue-green shutters.
Irish architect, Charles Blaney Cluskey, is believed to have designed these buildings.

• **(Richardson)-Owens-Thomas House Museum and Regency Shop** (c. 1819), 124 Abercorn Street. (912) 233-9743.
Renowned Regency house, designed by William Jay.
Just after Christmas, 1817, the young English architect, William Jay, reached Savannah and supervised construction of the house he had designed for cotton broker Richard Richardson. This outstanding example of Regency architecture is one of several important houses designed by Jay before he left the United States about 1824. In 1825, the Marquis de Lafayette visited Savannah and spoke from this glorious house. It is a

memorable experience to stand in the dining room on a sunny day with sunlight pouring through amber glass onto silver, brass, and mahogany. Miss Meta Thomas, granddaughter of a previous owner, George W. Owens, willed the house to the Telfair Academy of Arts and Sciences for a house museum. The house and even the kitchen below, have period furnishings. Visiting hours are 10 a.m.-5 p.m. Tues.-Sat. and 2-5 p.m. on Sun. afternoon. Guided tours begin as late as 4:30 p.m., and there's good browsing in the Regency Gift Shop. Admission. Closed Mon. and major holidays.

DIRECTIONS: Exit square, still on State Street, headed west (cross Drayton Street) to Wright Square.

Wright Square

Originally, this was Percival Square, in honor of the colonists' best friend in Parliament, the Right Honorable John Lord Viscount Percival, Earl of Egmont, and president of the Trustees of the Georgia colony. This is the second of the four wards laid out by Oglethorpe himself, and is home to two important monuments. In the southeast quadrant is a granite boulder given by the Colonial Dames in honor of Chief Tomochichi, who was buried nearby in 1739 with Oglethorpe as a pall bearer. Centering the square are the pink Georgia marble columns of the monument to William Washington Gordon, founder and president of the Central of Georgia Railroad and grandfather of Juliette Gordon Low.

Points of interest:
1. United States Post Office and Court House
2. Old Chatham County Courthouse
3. Evangelical Lutheran Church of the Ascension

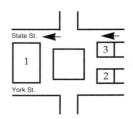

• **United States Post Office and Court House,** Wright Square Branch, (1898) 127 Bull Street.
Massive Georgia marble and granite building with intricate frieze under eaves.
Many architectural ideas are combined here. Put on your sunglasses and look up at the tower with its marble arches and intriguing details.

• **Old Chatham County Courthouse** (1889), 124 Bull Street.
Romanesque yellow brick and terra cotta on granite base.
The new Chatham County Courthouse is on Montgomery Street, and the old Court House is now the Administrative Legislative Center. William Gibbons Preston was the architect.

• **Evangelical Lutheran Church of the Ascension** (1879), Bull Street on Wright Square.
Soaring French Gothic spires; founded by Lutherans from Salzburg, Austria.
Salzburgers, led by Pastor John Martin Boltzius, gathered for the first time on Georgia soil in 1734, and so this parish was born. Although Pastor Boltzius and Oglethorpe sometimes disagreed, they believed that slavery should be banned in Georgia. Be sure to see Ascension's namesake stained glass window. This building was completed in 1879 with George B. Clarke as architect.

DIRECTIONS: Continue west on State Street (cross Whitaker Street) to Telfair Square.

Telfair Square

This became Telfair Square in the 1880s, in honor of the Telfairs, a family of scope and vision. (The original name was St. James Square after the square in London.) It's the fourth of Oglethorpe's original four squares.

Points of interest:
1. Telfair Museum of Art
2. Trinity United Methodist Church

• **Telfair Museum of Art** (building 1818), 121 Barnard Street, (912) 232-1177. Regency mansion designed by William Jay; statues in front of Phidias, Raphael, Rubens, Michelangelo, and Rembrandt.

Governor (in 1786) Edward Telfair had a son, Alexander, who recognized the architectural talent of young William Jay and commissioned him to design a house for the family. As specified in the will of Alexander's sister, Mary, the Telfair home became the Telfair Academy of Arts and Sciences in 1886. Needed expansion was overseen by architect, Detlef Lienau, who worked hard to preserve Jay's classical Greek design while providing space for exhibits, concerts, and lectures. The Telfair has an exciting schedule of events, plus the elegant, annual Telfair Ball and Auction in February. Open Tues.-Sat. 10 a.m.-5 p.m. and 2-5 p.m. on Sun. afternoons. Closed Mon. and major holidays.

• **Trinity United Methodist Church** (c. 1848), Barnard Street on Telfair Square.
Oldest Methodist church in Savannah; two Corinthian columns in front.

There's hand-hewn Georgia pine inside Trinity, built of stucco over Savannah grey brick along the lines of Trinity Chapel in London. John B. Hogg was architect. The "Mother Church of Methodism" has moved back in, following an enormous and devastating fire in 1991.

DIRECTIONS: Continue around square to State Street; go two blocks west, crossing Jefferson. Pause before turning right onto Montgomery Street to view:

• **New Chatham County Court House, on one of 3 squares lost to "progress."**
Liberty Square, named for the Liberty Boys of the American Revolution, has been all but obliterated by the Chatham County Courthouse and Jail (133 Montgomery Street). There's still a scrap of green, though, and it's marked on our map.

DIRECTIONS: Proceed north on Montgomery Street (cross Broughton Street) to Franklin Square.

Franklin Square

Laid out in 1790, Water Tank Square was later re-named to honor Benjamin Franklin, who served as the colonists' agent in London from 1768-1775. It was Franklin who sent seeds of the Chinese tallow tree to Noble Wimberly Jones in Georgia, with a note saying he hoped they'd flourish. Flourish they did, and now this tree even grows wild in the woods, with leaves like Chinese lanterns and "popcorn" seed pods for flower arrangers to harvest in autumn. Neglected a while, Franklin Square has recently been re-created and reinstated, bringing Savannah's total of squares to 21.

Points of interest:
1. New City Market
2. First African Baptist Church

• **New City Market**, 309 West St. Julian Street.
Formerly seed and feed warehouses, now a bustling beehive of restaurants, shops, and artists' studios.
The spacious courtyard is great for sipping espresso or just "people watching." Night life is alive and well with live music, plus indoor-outdoor dining or snacking. Come here to take a tour of Savannah by horse and carriage.

• **First African Baptist Church (1859)**, Montgomery Street on Franklin Square. **Oldest black church in North America; building constructed by slave hands.** First pastor here was George Leile, whose ministry began in 1775 and who was freed from slavery in 1777. First African Baptist and First Bryan Baptist both grew from this early congregation. George Leile baptized slave Andrew Bryan, who became second pastor at First African Baptist. Third pastor, Andrew Marshall, a slave for 50 of his 100 years, was in the pulpit here for 44 years. These men are pictured in stained glass windows. The marks of slavery can still be seen in this building, which was built by slave hands when their day's work was done. In the floor downstairs are breathing holes, said to be used by slaves fleeing to freedom via a secret tunnel from the church to the Savannah River; on pews in the balcony, enslaved artisans scratched in their African signatures—silent mementoes of souls in chains.

DIRECTIONS: Exit square onto Congress Street; (cross Jefferson Street) go two blocks east.

• **City Market Parking Garage (formerly Ellis Square)**
Once the site of Savannah's bustling City Market, torn down in 1954.
Instead of the vibrant and vigorous City Market, we have a

monument to the internal combustion engine—City Market Parking Garage. Even though City Market was razed, a spark of energy from the effort to save it burned on in the hearts of the seven women to whom this book is dedicated.

DIRECTIONS: Continue two more blocks east on Congress Street (cross Whitaker Street) to Johnson Square.

Johnson Square

Welcome to the navel of Savannah! Johnson Square was the first square laid out by Oglethorpe in 1733, named for Robert Johnson, friend and helper to Oglethorpe, and Governor of South Carolina in colonial days. It's the first of five squares on Bull Street. The obelisk is a monument to General Nathanael Greene, Revolutionary War hero and chief of staff to General George Washington. The cornerstone was laid by the Marquis de Lafayette on his trip to Savannah in 1825. Come to Johnson Square on a sunny day to find artists at work, live music, vendors selling hot dogs and lemonade, and office workers taking time for a chat or a snack.

• **Christ Church**, Episcopal, (1838), Bull Street on Johnson Square.
Third building on church site selected by Oglethorpe; "Mother Church of Georgia."
   The 1819 Revere bell that chimes before services bears these weighty words: "The living to the church I call, and to the grave I summon all." The classic Greek temple design came from architect, James Hamilton Couper. First minister to the colonists was the Reverend Dr. Henry Herbert, chaplain on the ship *Ann*. Later ministers included the Rev. John Wesley and the Rev. George Whitefield, impassioned preacher and founder in 1740 of Bethesda Orphan Home. Other "firsts" at Christ Church include America's first Sunday School and the first hymnal in English, both credited to John Wesley in 1736. (You may be interested to know that co-author Polly walked down the center aisle here in 1961 to marry Tim Cooper, and co-author

Emmeline was a staff member here until 1991.)

DIRECTIONS: Circle square to Congress Street; (cross Drayton Street) continue for 2 more blocks to Reynolds Square.

Reynolds Square

Mapped out in 1734 as Lower New Square, Reynolds Square was home to the Filature, where cocoons were brought and silk woven. Hopes for a flourishing silk industry were dashed when fire destroyed the Filature in 1758. The square was re-named for John Reynolds, first royal governor of Georgia. The statue, by sculptor Marshall Daugherty, is of the Rev. John Wesley and was dedicated by the Methodist Church in 1979. Mr. Wesley wears clerical vestments of the Church of England.

Points of interest:
1. **Lucas Theater for the Arts**
2. **Christ Church Parish House**
3. **Pink House**
4. **Oliver Sturges House**

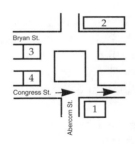

• **Lucas Theater for the Arts** (built 1921), corner of Abercorn and Congress Streets.
A 1920s movie palace, now being restored.
Arthur Lucas built this grand movie palace and for years the 4-story theater welcomed vaudeville's finest acts, as well as movies—first silent, then "talkies." Lucas Theater for the Arts was formed in 1989 with the goal of restoring the Lucas to its former splendor. If you can help, stop by the office at 24 Drayton Street, or call (912) 232-1696.

• **Christ Church Parish House**, 18 Abercorn Street.
(912) 232-4131.
Fourteen arched windows on a former cigar factory at corner of Abercorn and Bryan Streets.

Who knows how many stogies were rolled in this 4-story stucco-over-brick building when it housed the Cortez Cigar Company. Christ Church bought it in 1940 for offices and for the Sunday School begun by the Rev. John Wesley in 1736, the first in America. Enter through the 2-story building at the back of the garden, added later and named for the Rev. Francis Bland Tucker, D.D., rector of Christ Church from 1945-67. Beloved Dr. Tucker is remembered as "priest, poet, scholar, and significant contributor to English hymnody." The hungry and homeless come here for lunch Mon.-Fri. through Emmaus House, combined outreach project of a number of parishes and denominations.

• **Pink House**, or Habersham House (c. 1789), 23 Abercorn Street.
One of few buildings to survive the inferno of 1796 when over 200 houses were destroyed.
Built for "Liberty Boy" James Habersham, Jr., this house brightens the neighborhood with rose-pink stucco. Toward the end of the Civil War, it was headquarters for Union General Zebulon York; now it is a restaurant and tavern. Notice the Palladian window above the columned entrance.

• **Oliver Sturges House** (c. 1818), 27 Abercorn Street.
Masterful masonry with earthquake rods, dolphin downspouts.
Oliver Sturges, who built this house, was one of those who met here with Captain Moses Rogers to plan the landmark voyage in 1819 of the *SS Savannah*, the first steamship to cross the Atlantic. Now this exceptional brick structure houses the executive offices of a newspaper publishing corporation.

DIRECTIONS: Continue on Congress Street for two blocks to Warren Square.

Warren Square

This square was named for General Joseph Warren,

Revolutionary War hero, who died in the Battle of Bunker Hill in 1775. Warren and neighboring Washington Square comprise the first extension of Oglethorpe's original four, then six, squares. They were added in 1790.

Points of interest:
1. **John David Mongin House**
2. **22 Habersham Street**

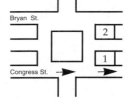

• **John David Mongin House** (1793), 24 Habersham Street.
Research by historian Walter Charlton Hartridge tells that Mr. Mongin was a planter of Sea Island cotton whose father-in-law lived at Bloody Point on Daufuskie Island. The Mongins inherited the Daufuskie property, but preferred to live here on Warren Square. The house served both as rectory for Christ Church and as a hospital when yellow fever struck Savannah in 1876.

• **22 Habersham Street**, (1790).
Mustard-toned frame house; escaped terrible fire of 1796.
This house is one of the few not consumed by the fire that swept through Savannah in 1796. The inferno began in "Mr. Gromet's bake house," gobbling more than 200 houses in four hours.

DIRECTIONS: Continue around square (cross Price Street) and stay on Congress Street for two more blocks to Washington Square.

Washington Square

Added in 1790 with Warren Square, Washington Square once bordered the Trustees' Garden in those early days and was known as Eastern Common. The square was named to honor General George Washington, the first president of the United States.

Points of interest:
1. Hampton Lillibridge House
2. International Seamen's House

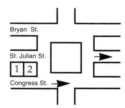

DIRECTIONS: Circle square to St. Julian Street. Pause to see:

• **Hampton Lillibridge House** (c. 1796), second house from square, 507 East Saint Julian Street, behind International Seamen's House.
Widow's walk atop gambrel roof on a grey frame house, rumored to be haunted.
Black and white trim accent the house built by New Jersey native, Hampton Lillibridge. It has long been known as a haunted house because of strange noises and weird happenings. Even after the Bishop of Georgia performed a rite of exorcism, the sound of clanking chains was heard. Of late, though, all has been peaceful here.

• **International Seamen's House**, 25 Houston Street.
Shady front porch with American flag; a welcome sight to seamen.
Seafaring men here in Georgia's state port come to Seaman's House to find warm hospitality, plus games, piano and guitars, television, and the Holy Bible in 30 languages. Chaplains visit all incoming vessels.

DIRECTIONS: Turn east on St. Julian Street; turn left on East Broad Street. To your right is Trustees' Garden Village.

Trustees' Garden Village

• **Trustees' Garden Village**, beginning at East Broad and Bay Streets.
Originally 10 acres of experimental garden for the colonists——now a residential delight.
Here are examples of the trail-blazing creativity of Mr. and

Mrs. H. Hansell Hillyer. In 1945, Mr. Hillyer was president of Savannah Gas Company. His wife, Mary, saw the possibilities in the rundown buildings around the old gasworks, the area that once was the country's first agricultural experiment station. Skeptical glances became smart salutes as Mrs. Hillyer transformed slum dwellings into snappy apartments, demonstrating (before the founding of Historic Savannah Foundation, Inc.) that historic preservation is a good investment. In 1960, Mary Hillyer was honored by the Georgia Historical Society, Historic Savannah, and the Savannah Jaycettes.

Shops and restaurants make up most of Bishop's Court, so named because the headquarters of the Episcopal Diocese of Georgia is here. This, too, is the site of Fort Savannah, built during the Revolutionary War and later re-named Fort Wayne in honor of General "Mad Anthony" Wayne.

DIRECTIONS: Past Trustees' Garden, turn right on Bay Street; turn left at railroad crossing onto River Street. As you drive along the river, to your right will be:

• **Statue of Florence Martus**, the "Waving Girl". **Bronze by Felix de Weldon, who also sculpted the Iwo Jima monument in Washington, D.C.** For fifty years, until 1931, Miss Martus lived on Elba Island with her brother, George, who tended warning lights along the Savannah River. Waving a white handkerchief by day, a lantern by night, she is said to have greeted every ship entering the Savannah harbor. She became known the wide world over as "The Waving Girl" and ships answered her wave with a "moo" of the horn, a wave, and often a letter. Some say she longed to greet a seafaring lover. The Altrusa Club gave this statue of Florence and her dog to the city. Behind the statue is William G. Morrell Park, named in honor of the Savannahian who headed the Savannah Park and Tree Commission for years.

DIRECTIONS: To the left will be:
• **Ships of the Sea Museum,** enter from 503 East River Street or 504 East Bay Street. (912) 232-1511.
Four floors of maritime mystique, not to be missed!
   Models on display here include Oglethorpe's ship, the *Ann*; the nuclear ship *NS Savannah*; and many more. There are prints and paintings, anchors, mastheads, plus scrimshaw and other collectibles. Open 10 a.m.-5 p.m. daily except major holidays. Admission.

DIRECTIONS: Turn left at Lincoln Ramp to Bay Street.

END OF TOUR

RIVER STREET AND BAY STREET TOUR

   This area exploded like a cotton boll after the invention of the cotton gin in 1793. More cotton production meant more shipping, so these multi-storied buildings began popping up on Savannah's shoreline for use as cotton warehouses. About the same time—the 1840s—the sandy bluff was faced with masonry. Ballast stones, used for weight in trading ships on the trip back from England, were used to build the picturesque ramps and walls between Bay Street and the river. Bustling River Street is fun for all ages with "First Saturday" festivals each month and free concerts in spring and autumn by the Savannah Symphony Orchestra. There are shops, museums, hotels, galleries, restaurants, riverboats, even candy factories that give free samples of pecan pralines and goober brittle! Free and paid parking.

DIRECTIONS: If driving, this tour begins on Rossiter Street behind Emmet Park, where the Savannah Panorama concluded. However, the best alternative is to park on River or Bay Street and walk.

• **Emmet Park**, from East Broad to Lincoln Street.
Honors Robert Emmet, Irish orator and patriot.
    Beneath this verdant vista is an Indian burial mound, called Indian Hill by the colonists. At the eastern tip of Emmet Park is Savannah's harbor light, installed in 1852 as a guide to mariners, warning them to steer clear of the spot where the British scuttled vessels during the American Revolution.

• **Factors' Row**, warehouses from East Broad to Bull Street.
Former cotton warehouses, usually five stories high when viewed from the river, and two stories high on Bay Street.
    These ex-cotton warehouses on Factors' Row were constructed in the first half of the 19th century, in the cotton boom that followed the invention of the cotton gin. Cotton orders followed a vertical path downward, from office to warehouse to a ship in the river. Offices, shops, hotels, and restaurants abound on the three levels that once served as offices, warehouses, and loading zones for cotton merchants, called factors.

• **Chatham Artillery Monument**, Emmet Park.
Commemorates Georgia military unit formed in 1786.
    "Soldiers in war; Patriots in Peace" is their motto. The famed Chatham Artillery Punch, a potent combination of rum, brandy, champagne, and other lethal liquids, is a weapon in its own right!

• **Vietnam Memorial**, Emmet Park near Price Street.
Tablet with names of Chatham County men and women killed in Vietnam.
    Benches invite us to stop and remember the terrible conflict that took 58,000 American lives. A helmet, rifle and combat boots are mute companions to the roster of names. The ground around is paved with bricks bearing the names of those who

helped to finance the building of this monument.

• **Celtic Cross of the Georgia Hussars,** Emmet Park near Lincoln.
Organized in 1736 by James Oglethorpe.
Oglethorpe organized the Georgia Hussars for protection against the Indians and the Spaniards. They have fought for Georgia since Colonial times and are still active in the Georgia Army National Guard.

• **Salzburger Monument,** on Bay Street at the end of Emmet Park near the Lincoln Street ramp.
Carved from green serpentine from Austria's highest mountain, in memory of the Salzburg Lutherans who fled to Georgia in 1734 to escape religious persecution.
The monument bears these words in German and English: "Denied their religious freedom, they were forced to flee their homeland." It depicts a Salzburg family in flight. The sculptor was Anton Thuswaldner, who was present for the dedication ceremony in 1994.

DIRECTIONS: Exit Emmet Park at light at Lincoln Street; turn right onto Bay into right lane headed west.

• **Old City Exchange Bell,** Bay Street at Drayton Street.
A cupola with a bell—all that remains from the old City Exchange, built in 1799.
The Old City Exchange (City Hall) was replaced in 1906 by our present, golden-domed City Hall. The iron urns on either side were brought to Savannah by Henry Rootes Jackson when he was United States ambassador to Austria.

OLD EXCHANGE AND CITY HALL

• **Cotton Exchange** (now Solomon's Lodge) (1886), 100 East Bay Street.
Look high up for completion date, molded in terra cotta.

William Gibbons Preston was architect for this decorative delight, our finest example of Romanesque architecture. The Cotton Exchange was the hub of the cotton industry in the 1890s and was the first U.S. building to be built over a street, using the principle of "air rights." Around the winged lion in front are iron medallions with famous faces, salvaged from the Wetter House when it was pulled down on Oglethorpe Avenue and Martin Luther King, Jr. Boulevard, then West Broad Street.

• **Historical marker near where the University of Georgia was chartered.**
In a nearby coffee house in 1785, the Assembly of Georgia voted to establish a public institution of higher education. This was the first charter for a state university to be issued in the United States.

• **Washington Guns.**
Pair of bronze cannon captured at Yorktown, known as "George and Martha"; given to the Chatham Artillery by President George Washington after his visit to Savannah in 1791.

• **United States Custom House**, (c. 1848), 1 East Bay Street, across Bay Street.
Soaring columns of Georgia granite at the entrance to the Savannah office of the Customs Service, United States Treasury Department.
The Greek Revival design was drawn by architect John S. Norris.

• **Savannah City Hall** (1905), north side of Bay at Bull Street.
A golden dome atop Savannah's legislative center, at the beginning of Bull Street.

What a view there must be from the top of Savannah's City Hall! Hyman W. Witcover was the architect. This building replaces the 1799 City Exchange, razed in 1904 to the sorrow of Mayor Thomas Gamble.

• **Oglethorpe Bench**, Bay Street just west of City Hall.
A marble bench at the spot where Oglethorpe pitched his tent on February 12, 1733.

Oglethorpe's tent is visible in Peter Gordon's 1734 map of the new colony, prepared for the Trustees at Oglethorpe's request.

DIRECTIONS: If driving, get in the right lane to descend to River Street via the Barnard Street ramp. If walking, there's a challenging flight of stairs. The white blocks on this ramp were hewn from the White Cliffs of Dover.

• **Rousakis Plaza**, River Street at the bottom of the Barnard Street ramp.
A brick promenade named for a Savannah mayor, who was

also known as "Mr. Basketball" in the 1940s.

Watch for the River Street Rambler, a freight train that rumbles regularly down these tracks.

DIRECTIONS: A landmark on the trip east on River Street is the underpass of the Hyatt-Regency Hotel. Return to Bay Street via the ramp (or stairs) just beyond the statue of the Waving Girl. (See Savannah Panorama for more information about the Waving Girl and the Ships of the Sea Museum.)

END OF TOUR

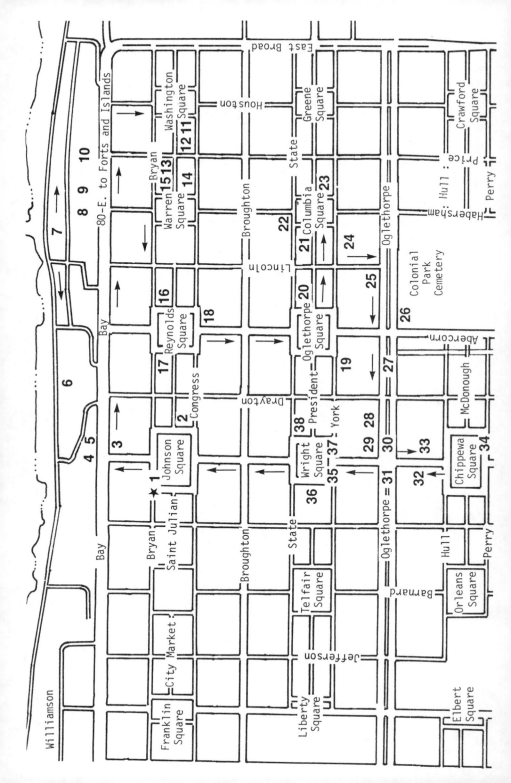

"HITTING HIGH SPOTS" WALKING TOUR

This one hour minimum walking tour in Savannah's historic district can begin at any point. Refer to map for numbered sites and sights. (More detailed descriptions can be found in the Savannah Panorama section.)

Johnson Square was the first square laid out by our founder, James Edward Oglethorpe. **Monument** (1) is to General Nathanael Greene, General George Washington's valued aide in the Revolutionary War. **Christ Church (Episcopal)** (2) is the "Mother Church of Georgia," where John Wesley established the first Sunday School in the USA. At Bull and Bay Streets is the **U.S. Custom House (3)** with six monolithic granite columns. Across Bay Street, gold-domed **City Hall** (4) faces southward over the five squares on Bull Street. **Washington Guns** (5), taken from Cornwallis at Yorktown, were given to the Chatham Artillery by George Washington. They are affectionately known as "George and Martha."

Cotton Exchange (6), now Solomon's Lodge, was built over a public road. Fence around winged lion has medallions with famous faces. **Factors' Row (or Factors' Walk)** (7) was offices and warehouses when cotton was "king". **Emmet Park** has a **Celtic Cross** (8), **Vietnam Memorial** (9), and monument to Georgia's **Chatham Artillery** (10). **Savannah River** is in view with River Street below for shopping and dining.

Washington Square has many private houses with interesting architectural details. **International Seamen's House** (11) offers southern hospitality to visiting seamen. **The Hampton Lillibridge House** (12), with widow's walk on gambrel roof, has a spooky reputation. **426 East St. Julian Street** (13) was built in the late 1700s. This is where Jane DeVeaux had a secret school for slave children before the Civil War. On the east side of Warren Square are **22 and 24 Habersham Street** (14 and 15), two restored, 18th-century clapboard houses.

In **Reynolds Square**, the **Rev. John Wesley** (16) seems to be delivering a sermon. He was the founder of Methodism. **Pink House** (17) was former home of James Habersham, Jr., one of the Liberty Boys who opposed the controls of King George III. The **Lucas Theater** (18) is the focus of a mammoth effort to make this 1920s movie palace sparkle once again. On **Oglethorpe Square** is the **Urban Health Center** (19), a large, beige building that once was the U. S. Marine Hospital. The **Owens-Thomas House** (20) is a nationally-known example of Regency architecture. Lafayette spoke to townspeople in 1825 from this house.

On **Columbia Square** is the Victorian **Kehoe House** (21), built by the owner of Kehoe Iron Works for his large, Irish family (became a funeral home, was later co-owned by football legend, Joe Namath, and is now an inn.); Federal style **Davenport House** (22) was saved from destruction by the seven women who founded the Historic Savannah Foundation, Inc., and to whom this guidebook is dedicated. In **Columbia Square** is a **cast iron fountain** (23) from Wormsloe Plantation, home of Noble Jones, one of the original passengers on the *Ann* with Oglethorpe. **Orange tree gate** (24) was forged by Ivan Bailey, metalsmith, who now lives in Atlanta. Star shapes mark the ends of earthquake rods, installed in houses to diffuse tremors. Numbers 230-244 Oglethorpe Avenue are known as **Marshall Row** (25). Pulitzer Prize-winning author and poet, Conrad Aiken, lived with his wife, Mary, in No. 230 when he came back to Savannah in 1962.

Gates of Colonial Park Cemetery (26) were given by the Daughters of the American Revolution. Here are the graves of famous duelists Button Gwinnett, signer of the Declaration of Independence from Georgia, and Lachlan McIntosh. Squares once were numbered, so when **"Big Duke," the fire bell** (27), rang to announce a fire, everyone counted the bongs to locate the blaze. At **14 East Oglethorpe** (28) once lived Juliette Gordon Low's cousin, Nina Anderson Pape, founder and headmistress of Pape School. Sixteen of her students became this country's first Girl Scouts. Pape School became Savannah Country Day School in the 1950s. Next door, **Wayne-Gordon House Museum** (29), is the birthplace of Juliette Gordon Low, founder in 1912 of the Girl Scouts of The United States of America. It is now the Juliette Gordon Low National Girl Scout Center. **Scottish Monument** (30) honors the bravery of Scots in Georgia in defending the colony against the Spaniards to the south. **Mordecai Sheftall Monument** (31) marks the site of the oldest Jewish burial ground in the colony.

At **Independent Presbyterian Church** (32), a promising young attorney, Woodrow Wilson, was married to Ellen Axson, the pastor's granddaughter. Burned to the ground in 1889, the church was rebuilt using the original plans. **Chatham Academy Building** (33) now houses administrative offices of Chatham-Savannah Public Schools. In **Chippewa Square** stands **General James Edward Oglethorpe** (34). Lettering on the monument tells his courageous story.

Wright Square was named for Sir James Wright, last of three royal governors of Georgia. **Monument** (35) commemorates William Washington Gordon, founder of the Central of Georgia Railroad. **Branch of the U. S. Post Office** (36) is on the west side of the square. **Granite boulder** (37) was given by Colonial Dames in memory of Tomochichi, chief of the Yamacraw tribe of Creek Indians, and trusted friend of Oglethorpe.

Evangelical Lutheran Church of the Ascension (38) was established in 1741 by Salzburgers from Austria, led here by Pastor John Martin Boltzius to escape religious persecution.

This tour ends with a short walk north on Bull Street to your starting point, Johnson Square.

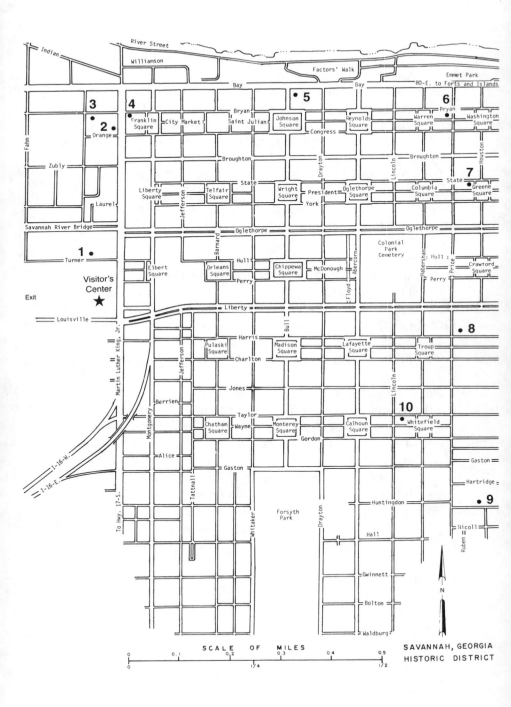

SCALE OF MILES

SAVANNAH, GEORGIA
HISTORIC DISTRICT

AFRICAN-AMERICAN HERITAGE DRIVING TOUR

Although slavery was banned in the Georgia colony, the colonists hired blacks from South Carolina to build their wooden houses. When the ban on slavery was lifted in 1750, the number of African-Americans increased greatly and slaves became the key to success in the production of cotton and rice, as well as Savannah grey bricks and ironwork.

Black volunteers from Haiti came to aid the Americans during the Siege of Savannah in 1779. Among these was Henri Christophe, who later became free Haiti's first ruler in the early 1800s. Free blacks operated the fire stations in Savannah in this same period.

Until slavery ended in 1865, the teaching of reading and writing to slaves and their children was forbidden. Underground schools operated secretly with courageous teachers including Jane DeVeaux, Susie King Taylor, James Porter, the Rev. James M. Simms, and Julien Fromontin.

After slavery was abolished through the Emancipation Proclamation and the Civil War, people of African descent continued to make positive contributions to life in Savannah and continue to do so today. The following tour will tell of people and places that are important in this history. (More detailed information on many of these sites can be found in the Savannah Panorama Tour.)

1. **Turner Memorial**, on Turner Street just north of the Visitor's Center, near Martin Luther King, Jr., Boulevard. This memorial monument honors Bishop Henry McNeal Turner, appointed by

President Abraham Lincoln in 1863 as the first black chaplain in the Union army. After the Civil War, he joined the A.M.E. (African Methodist Episcopal) Church, in which he was made a bishop in 1880.

2. **William Scarbrough House**, 41 Martin Luther King, Jr., Boulevard, designed by William Jay and once used as a school for children of African descent.

3. **First Bryan Baptist Church**, 575 West Bryan Street, part of the oldest black congregation in North America, established in 1777 by George Leile.

4. **First African Baptist Church**, 31 Montgomery Street, on Franklin Square, built by black slaves in 1859.

5. **U.S. Custom House**, 1 East Bay Street. Colonel John H. DeVeaux, free-born into a family from Santo Domingo and educated in underground schools in Savannah, founded the newspaper *Colored Tribune* (later *Savannah Tribune*) in 1875. Later he was appointed U.S. Collector of Customs, the first black man to occupy this high office. Sol C. Johnson took over his duties at the *Tribune*.

6. **426 East Saint Julian Street**, once an underground school for black children with Jane DeVeaux as teacher.

7. **Second African Baptist Church**, 123 Houston Street, where General Sherman visited just after the Civil War, allotting "40 acres and a mule" to newly-freed slaves.

8. **Beach Institute**, African-American Cultural Center, 502 East Harris Street at Price Street. (912) 234-8000. Originally a school for black children after the Civil War, Beach Institute is now a

museum where the Ulysses Davis collection of wood carvings can be seen. Established just after the Civil War on land purchased by Alfred Beach, editor of *Scientific American* magazine, Beach Institute was staffed by white teachers from the north who came to teach newly-freed black children. Today, the Institute offers a full schedule of programs and exhibits, plus a gift shop. Hours are 12-5 p.m. Tues.-Sun. Admission.

9. **King-Tisdell Cottage Museum**, 514 East Huntingdon Street, (912) 234-8000. Dedicated to the preservation of African-American history and culture, this museum contains artwork, documents, and furnishings typical of a coastal black dwelling of the 1890s. The 1896 frame building features intricate "gingerbread" woodwork in the "Wheel and Spindle" pattern. Be sure to ask about the symbolism in the fountain in the garden, created by metalsmith Ivan Bailey. The King-Tisdell Cottage was saved from demolition by the Savannah-Yamacraw Branch Association for the Study of Afro-American Life and History, which is now working to establish a Civil Rights Museum at 460 Martin Luther King, Jr., Boulevard. Hours are 12-4:30 p.m. daily; other times by appointment. Admission. For an in-depth chronicle of African-American history, make a reservation here for the **Negro Heritage Trail Tour**, offered Mon.-Sat. 1 p.m and 3 p.m. Leaves from the Savannah Visitor's Center. (912) 234-8000. Admission.

10. **First Congregational Church**, United Church of Christ, 421 Habersham Street, founded in 1869.

Not on this tour but nearby and of interest: **Savannah State College**, at Thunderbolt, established in 1840 in Athens as the Georgia State Industrial College for Colored Youths.

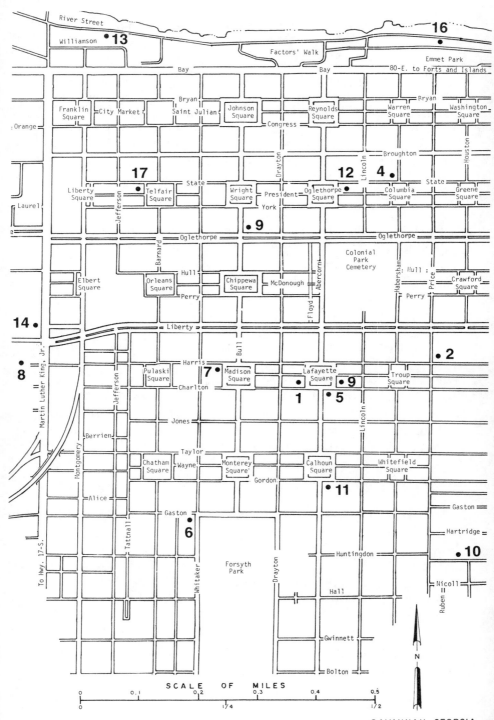

SAVANNAH, GEORGIA
HISTORIC DISTRICT

MUSEUMS AND HISTORIC HOUSES

1. Andrew Low House Museum, 329 Abercorn Street; (912) 233-6854. Handsomely-furnished Georgia headquarters of The National Society of The Colonial Dames of America in the state of Georgia; designed in 1848 by architect John S. Norris for cotton broker Andrew Low; Juliette Gordon Low founded Girl Scouts here in 1912. Open Mon.-Sat. 10:30 a.m.-4 p.m.; Sun., 12 noon-4 p.m. Closed Thurs. Donations: Adults, $5; students ages 12–18 and members of tour groups, $2; children ages 11-6, $1; aged 5 and under, free.

2. Beach Institute African-American Cultural Arts Center, 502 East Harris Street; (912) 234-8000. Established in 1865 to educate newly-freed black citizens; exhibits include wood carvings of folk artist Ulysses Davis. Open Tues.-Sat. noon-5 p.m. Admission: $3. WCA.

3. Bethesda Home for Boys — Museum and Chapel; 9520 Ferguson Avenue; (912) 351-2040. A wealth of Bethesda history and mementoes. Museum hours: Mon.-Fri., 9 a.m.-5 p.m.; chapel, 9 a.m.-5 p.m. daily. Free.

4. Davenport House Museum and Gift Shop, 324 East State Street; (912) 236-8097. Begun in 1818 by builder Isaiah Davenport as his dwelling; rescued from demolition in 1955, thus sparking the organization of Historic Savannah Foundation, Inc. Open daily 10 a.m.-4 p.m.; Admission: adults, $4; ages 6-18, $3; under age 6, free. (No charge to visit shop or garden.)

5. Flannery O'Connor Childhood Home, 207 East Charlton Street; (912) 233-6014. Home of Edward and Regina O'Connor, whose only child, Mary Flannery, became one of America's most outstanding authors. Her works include *Wise Blood, The Violent Bear It Away,* and *A Good Man Is Hard to Find.* She received the National Short Story Award three times as well as the O'Henry Book Award. Open Fri.-Sun. 1-4 p.m. free.

6. Georgia Historical Society, 501 Whitaker Street, (912) 651-2128. Research library and archives specializing in historic records. Open Tues.–Fri., 10 a.m.–5 p.m.; Sat. 9 a.m.–3 p.m., Free. WCA via elevator in garden.

7. Green-Meldrim House Museum, on Madison Square; (912) 233-3845. Gothic Revival mansion completed in 1853 by architect-builder John S. Norris; headquarters of General Sherman when he occupied Savannah toward end of Civil War; now parish house of St. John's Episcopal Church. The black walnut woodwork and curved stair are worth seeing. Open Tues., Thurs., Fri., and Sat., 10 a.m.-4 p.m. Admission: adults, $3; ages 6-18, $l; under age 6, free.

8. Historic Railroad Shops, 601 West Harris Street, (912) 651-6823. Built in 1850s, one of the few remaining railroad complexes in the nation. Open, Mon.–Sat. 10 a.m.–4 p.m.; Sun. noon–4 p.m., admission adults, $2.50, seniors, children, students $2.

9. Juliette Gordon Low Girl Scout Center, 142 Bull Street; (912) 233-4501. Birthplace of Juliette Gordon Low, founder of Girl Scouts; furnished to reflect her life in the 1870s and 1880s, before marriage. Open Mon.-Sat. (closed Wed.) 10 a.m.-4 p.m.; Sun. 12:30-4:30 p.m. Admission: adults, $5; students, $3. Discount for Girl Scouts.

10. King-Tisdell Cottage Museum, 514 East Huntingdon Street; (912) 234-8000. 1896 Victorian cottage; now a museum of African-American culture. Open Tues.-Fri. 1-4:30 p.m.; Sat. 1-4 p.m. Admission: $2.50.

11. Massie Heritage Interpretation Center, 207 East Gordon Street; (912) 651-7022. Built as a public school for needy children; now a resource center for living history. Open Mon.-Fri. 9 a.m.-4 p.m. Admission: $1.

12. Owens-Thomas House Museum (Regency Shop), 124 Abercorn Street; (912) 233-9743. Designed by English architect William Jay; Regency architecture and furnishings. Open Tues.-Sat. 10 a.m.-5 p.m.; Sun.-Mon. 2-5 p.m. Admission: adults, $5; students, $3; ages 6-12, $2; age 5 and under, free.

13. River Street Train Museum, 315 West River Street; (912) 233-6175. Guided tours through antique toy train displays and memorabilia. Open Mon.-Sat. 11 a.m.-5:30 p.m.; Sun. 1-6 p.m. Admission: Adults, $1.50; ages 5-12,$.50; under age 5, free. WCA with 2 steps.

14. Savannah History Museum, 303 Martin Luther King, Jr., Boulevard; (912) 238-1779. Former Central of Georgia Railway passenger station; artifacts, displays, video presentations of Savannah history. Open daily, 9 a.m.-5 p.m. Admission: adults,

$3; students, $2.50; ages 6-12, $l.75; under age 6, free. WCA.

15. Savannah Science Museum, 4405 Paulsen Street; (912) 355-6705. Hands-on exhibits of natural and physical sciences, astronomy. Open Tues.-Sat. 10 a.m.-5 p.m.; Sun. 2-5 p.m. Admission: age 12 and over, $3; ages 3-11 and seniors, $2; free for age 2 and under, members, and on 2nd Sun. of each month. WCA.

16. Ships of the Sea Museum, 503 East River Street or 504 East Bay Street; (912) 232-1511. Large collection of ship models and maritime memorabilia, located in one of the first waterfront buildings to be restored. Many enjoy the museum's Ship-in-a-Bottle collection of over 75 miniature ships. Open daily, 10 a.m.-5 p.m. Admission: adults, $3; ages 7-12, $1.50; age 6 and under, free.

17. Telfair Museum of Art, 121 Barnard Street; (912) 232-1177. Savannah's art museum in Telfair family mansion, designed by William Jay. Open Tues.-Sat. 10 a.m.-5 p.m.; Sun.–Mon. 2-5 p.m. Admission: adults, $3; students and seniors, $1; ages 6-12, $.50; age 5 and under, free. WCA.

18. Tybee Lighthouse and Museum, 18 miles east of Savannah on Highway 80; (912) 786-5801. Exhibits and video presentation of Tybee history; doll and gun displays in 1898 fortification. Open daily Apr. 1-first Mon. in Sept. (closed Tues.) 10 a.m.-6 p.m.; first Wed. in Sept.-Mar. 31 (closed Tues.), Mon.-Fri. noon-4 p.m.; Sat.-Sun. 10 a.m.-4 p.m. Admission: age 12 and over, $2.50; seniors, $1.50; ages 6-12, $.75; age 5 and under, free.

19. Wormsloe Historic Site, 7601 Skidaway Road; (912) 353-3023. Plantation home of Noble Jones, who came on the *Ann* with Oglethorpe; museum with gift shop, video presentation. Open Tues.-Sat. 9 a.m.-5 p.m.; Sun. 2-5:30 p.m. Admission: adults, $2; ages 6-18, $1; age 5 and under, free with parents, $.25 cents in groups. WCA.

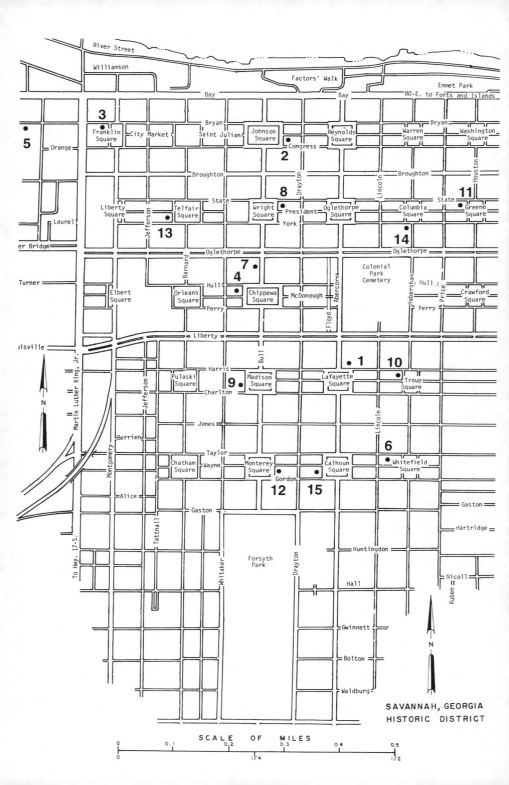

SAVANNAH, GEORGIA
HISTORIC DISTRICT

HISTORIC CHURCHES

For more details on historic churches, consult the Savannah Panorama tour.

1. Cathedral of Saint John the Baptist — Abercorn Street at Lafayette Square; (912) 233-4709. Roman Catholic Mass on Sat. at 5:30 p.m.; Sun. at 8 a.m., 10 a.m., and 11:30 a.m. Visit daily, 9:30 a.m.-5 p.m.

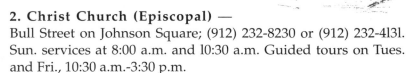

2. Christ Church (Episcopal) — Bull Street on Johnson Square; (912) 232-8230 or (912) 232-4l3l. Sun. services at 8:00 a.m. and l0:30 a.m. Guided tours on Tues. and Fri., 10:30 a.m.-3:30 p.m.

3. First African Baptist Church — Montgomery Street on Franklin Square; (912) 233-6597. Sun. service at ll:30 a.m. Visit Fri., 10 a.m.-2 p.m., or by appointment.

4. First Baptist Church — Bull Street on Chippewa Square; (912) 234-2671. Sun. service at 11 a.m. Call for time to visit.

5. First Bryan Baptist Church — 575 West Bryan Street; (912) 232-5526. Sun. service at ll a.m. Call for time to visit.

6. First Congregational Church — Habersham Street on

Whitefield Square; (912) 236-6521. Sun. service at 10 a.m. Call for time to visit.

7. Independent Presbyterian Church — Bull Street and Oglethorpe Avenue; (912) 236-3346. Services Sun. at ll a.m. and 5:30 p.m. Summer Sun. evening service on Talahi Island; call for directions.

8. Evangelical Lutheran Church of the Ascension — Bull Street on Wright Square; (912) 232-4151. Services Sun. at 8:30 a.m. and ll a.m. Visit Mon.-Fri., 8:30 a.m.-4:30 p.m.

ST. JOHN'S CHURCH, SAVANNAH, GEORGIA.

9. Saint John's Episcopal Church — Bull Street on Madison Square; (912) 232-1251. Services Sun. at 8 a.m., 10:30 a.m., and 12 noon. Visit Tues., Thurs., Fri., or Sat., 10 a.m.-4 p.m.

10. Savannah Baptist Center — Habersham Street on Troup Square; (912) 232-1033. Sun. service at 11 a.m. Visit Mon.–Thurs., 8:30 a.m.–4:30 p.m.

11. Second African Baptist Church — Houston Street on Greene Square; (912) 233-6163. Sun. service at 11 a.m. Call for time to visit.

12. Temple Mickve Israel — Bull Street on Monterey Square; (912) 233-1547. Services Fri. at 8:15 p.m.; Sat. at ll a.m. Visit Mon.-Fri., 10 a.m.-noon and 2-4 p.m.

13. Trinity United Methodist Church — Barnard Street on Telfair Square; (912) 233-4766. Sun. service at 11 a.m. Visit Mon.-Fri., 9 a.m.-3 p.m.

14. Unitarian Universalist Church — York Street on Columbia Square; (912) 234-0980. Sun. services at 9 a.m. and 11 a.m.

15. Wesley Monumental United Methodist Church — Abercorn Street on Calhoun Square; (912) 232-0191. Sun. services at 8:30 a.m. and 11 a.m. Visit Mon.-Fri., 9 a.m.-4:30 p.m.

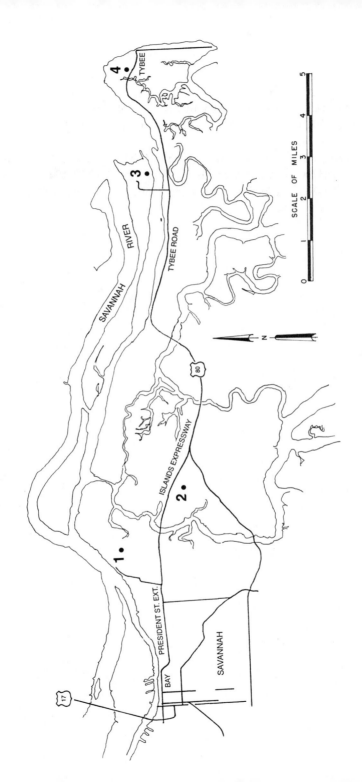

SCALE OF MILES

SAVANNAH RIVER

TYBEE ROAD

TYBEE

ISLANDS EXPRESSWAY

PRESIDENT ST. EXT.

BAY

SAVANNAH

N

0 1 2 3 4 5

80

17

FORTS AND ISLANDS EXCURSION

1. Fort Jackson — (912) 232-3945, 1 Fort Jackson Road.

DIRECTIONS: From the Visitor's Center, drive north on Martin Luther King, Jr., Boulevard; turn right onto Bay Street. Go east on Bay (which soon merges with Islands Expressway) for 2.7 miles, then follow the signs and cross the moat into Fort Jackson. Hours: 9 a.m.-5 p.m. daily. (Open until 7 p.m. Jul. 1-Aug. 15.) Admission: adults, $2.50; students, $2; under age 5, free. WCA.

This is the oldest fort still standing in Georgia. In 1775, during the Revolutionary War, an earthen battery was built here. The brick fort was begun in 1808 and manned during the War of 1812. Fort Jackson was most active as headquarters for Confederate defense of the Savannah River during the Civil War. Every ship entering the harbor passes here. Military exhibits and an audio-visual program are on display in the fort's casemates.

2. Oatland Island Education Center — (912) 897-3773, 711 Sandtown Road.

DIRECTIONS: Leaving the fort, turn left on Islands Expressway and continue east for 2.3 miles. On the right will be the Oatland Island sign. Hours: Mon.-Fri., 8:30 a.m.-5 p.m. Cash donations welcome. WCA.

Stroll the shady trails and watch wolves, bobcats, pumas, black bears, great bald eagles, and deer in their natural habitats. From a bridge, see basking alligators.

Two 1837 log cabins were moved to Oatland from north

Georgia. Bring a picnic and settle down on the 500-foot board-walk. You may see pelicans, great blue herons, woodpeckers, or long-legged egrets. Those mini-crab crustaceans are called "fiddler crabs," so named because the male of the species holds its huge, anterior claw the way a musician holds a "fiddle."

Trail maps are in the main building. In gnat season, bring a repellent.

3. Fort Pulaski National Monument and Museum — (912) 786-5787.

DIRECTIONS: Leaving Oatland Island, turn right and get back on Islands Expressway, (soon to join Highway 80); drive 7.7 miles to Fort Pulaski on the left. Hours: 8:30 a.m.-6:45 p.m. daily, June-Sept. 1; 8:30 a.m.-5:30 p.m., Sept. 2-May. Admission: adults, $2; ages 16 and under, free. WCA; Bookstore/museum.

Located on Cockspur Island at the mouth of the Savannah River, this masterpiece of masonry was built for coastal defense in the early 1800s. It bears the name of Count Casimir Pulaski, the gallant Polish cavalry officer who died in the Siege of Savannah. This was the first post for young Lieutenant Robert E. Lee when he finished the U. S. Military Academy at West Point.

Beyond the moat and portcullis, the five-sided fort encloses a 2.5-acre parade ground. With two tiers of guns and cannon, Confederate troops felt safe, snug, out of range of enemy artillery in the Civil War. The test came in 1862.

The Confederates knew that Union troops were installing cannon on Tybee Island, but they did not know that these were the new James and Parrott rifled cannon. When projectiles came crashing through the walls and into the powder magazine, Colonel Charles Olmstead surrendered the fort in April, 1862. Reading (in the museum) his letter to his wife after the surrender, one feels his anxiety and concern over his men and their thoughts of him.

The whole area covers 537 acres and is inviting for walking, driving, picnicking, or stretching out in the sun to watch the river.

4. Tybee Island (Savannah Beach), Fort Screven Museum, and Lighthouse. (912) 786-5801.

DIRECTIONS: Leaving Fort Pulaski, turn left onto Highway 80; continue east for 3.1 miles; turn left at traffic light and follow signs to the Tybee Museum.

The museum is tucked into a gun battery of Fort Screven, a fortification built in 1875 on the former site of the Union cannon that breached the walls of Fort Pulaski. Fort Screven saw service in the Spanish-American War and both World Wars.

A World War I submarine periscope in the museum gives a sweeping view of Tybee Island and the mouth of the Savannah River. Vivid dioramas and a film tell the story of Tybee history under seven flags—Oglethorpe's meeting with Tomochichi and Mary Musgrove, and Blackbeard the Pirate burying treasure on the island. (Tybee is a Euchee Indian word meaning salt.)

Tybee Lighthouse has 178 steps from deck to beacon, plus a superb view of Hilton Head, Daufuskie Island, and any ships entering the channel. Open daily, except Tues. Admission.

To see more of Tybee Island, continue on Highway 80 as it becomes Butler Avenue, which runs the full length of the island. In addition to everything the Atlantic Ocean has to offer, Tybee has restaurants, shopping, motels, and great spots to watch the sunset. Return by the same route, or consult map to return via Victory Drive.

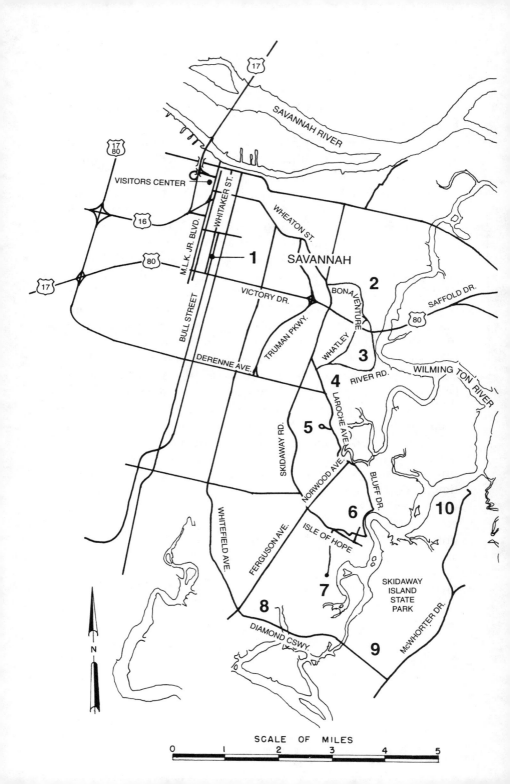

RIVERBANK RAMBLE

A 3-4 hour driving tour to places of interest on river and marsh.

DIRECTIONS: From the Visitor's Center, drive south on Martin Luther King, Jr. Boulevard three blocks to Liberty Street; turn left and go to the second light (at Whitaker Street); turn right and go to Park Avenue at the end of Forsyth Park; go left for one block; turn right onto Bull Street and proceed south through two lights to 36th Street. Look right to see:

1. Gingerbread House (1889) — 1921 Bull Street.

Cord Asendorf, grocer and owner, designed this intricate and unusual Victorian "gingerbread." It has been called a "two-tiered architectural confection." President Franklin Roosevelt was so entranced that he stopped his car so Sara, his mother, could get a proper look. The house can be spied in the background of many movies, including *Pals*, with George C. Scott and Don Ameche.

DIRECTIONS: Go south on Bull Street to Victory Drive (2nd light); left on Victory for 3 miles to Whatley Road; left on Whatley to stop sign; merge left onto Bonaventure Road. Soon on the right will be the impressive entrance to:

2. Bonaventure Cemetery — (912) 651-6843.

The name means "good fortune." In 1907, Savannah purchased the colonial plantation of the Tattnall family for use as a burying ground, ceding control of these riverside acres to the

Park and Tree Commission. In the spring, the moss-hung oaks, lavender and white wisteria, bridal white spirea, roses and azaleas make true the saying that visitors to Savannah are often taken to the cemetery!

The Lawton-Cunningham lot has two monuments of Italian marble—a figure of Christ and a young woman representing a member of the Lawton family who died just prior to her wedding day.

Many come, also, to visit the grave of Gracie Watson, daughter of the owners of the old Pulaski Hotel, which once stood where Morrison's Cafeteria stands today. In 1889, when she died of pneumonia at age six, Gracie was the darling of hotel guests and staff. 40 years later, Savannah sculptor John Walz carved her likeness in pristine Italian marble. Visitors often lay flowers in Gracie's lap to show that she's remembered with love.

Arrows point to Gracie's grave, as well as those of famed Savannah lyricist, Johnny Mercer, and Noble Jones, distinguished colonist who traveled on the *Ann* with Oglethorpe, and who died in Savannah just before the Declaration of Independence. Gates are open Mon.-Fri. 8 a.m.-5 p.m., Sat. 11 a.m.-2 p.m., Sun. 2-4 p.m.

DIRECTIONS: Leaving the cemetery, turn left onto Bonaventure Road (past Whatley Road). Cross Highway 80 to River Road in the town with the electrifying name of:

3. Thunderbolt.

This fishing and shrimping community on the Wilmington River was settled by Roger Lacy with a 500-acre grant from King George II. An Indian legend tells that fresh water sprang here from the spot where a thunderbolt of lightning struck the earth.

During the Revolutionary War, when the French in 1779 sent aid to the British-held city of Savannah, Count d'Estaing, the French commandant, encamped here on the bluff. Several riverbank restaurants look out over the shrimp boats and docks. The annual Blessing of the Fleet, held in May or June, is a colorful event. A priest sprinkles holy water on the shrimp boats, praying for a bountiful harvest. Arts and crafts are sold. Call (912) 354-5537 for details.

DIRECTIONS: Take River Road, which soon becomes Falligant; turn left onto Whatley, then right at the STOP sign. In spite of a sign that reads "No Thru Traffic," visitors are welcome at:

4. Savannah State College — (912) 356-2181 or 1-800-788-0478.

Established in 1890, Savannah State was then called Georgia State Industrial College for Colored Youths and was located in Athens, Georgia, before moving to Thunderbolt. In the beginning, there were four faculty members, four college students, and 60 elementary and secondary students. From this humble beginning grew an institution that's now the fifth largest in the Georgia university system.

Savannah State offers baccalaureate degrees, as well as associate of science and associate of arts degrees. There's a dual degree program in engineering with the Georgia Institute of Technology.

DIRECTIONS: Turn right at 2nd stop sign, then exit via gate; turn left onto Laroche Avenue to travel 1.4 miles through 2 lights. On the right is:

5. Majestic Oaks.

The name of this subdivision comes from the venerable oak tree just inside the entrance. Some believe that this gnarled, bearded Methuselah is 500 years old! If it could speak, what tales it might tell.

The Neighborhood Association maintains this giant as an "historic tree." Its canopy shades many a happy picnic and birthday party.

DIRECTIONS: Exit Majestic Oaks, turning right onto Laroche Avenue; after 1.9 miles, turn right onto Bluff Drive. Welcome to the waterfront community with the poignant name of:

6. Isle of Hope.

King George II in 1736 gave this high ground on the Skidaway River to three men of prominence: Noble Jones (who arrived with Oglethorpe) was given the 500 acres that are now Wormsloe Plantation; John Fallowfield, first bailiff, received the middle 500 acres; the rest was granted to the second bailiff, Henry Parker. The original name, Parkersburg, was changed to L'Ile d'Esperance (Isle of Hope) by Royalists seeking refuge during the French Revolution. This and other waterfront communities were havens for those fleeing yellow fever in Savannah, or just the summer heat. Now it's a choice residential area.

DIRECTIONS: At the end of Bluff Drive, turn right onto Noble Glen Drive to the end; left onto Diana Drive; right onto Richmond Drive, then merge into Skidaway Road. Soon on the left will be the entrance gate of:

7. Wormsloe Plantation — 7601 Skidaway Road; (912) 353-3023.

At Wormsloe, original owner Noble Jones planted grapes and mulberry trees for silk production. He also planted cotton and rice, and raised cattle. He cut a three-mile path through the woods to the Rev. George Whitefield's orphan house, Bethesda. After centuries of single family ownership, Wormsloe (except for the house, library and gardens) became the property of the State of Georgia in 1973.

An awesome avenue lined with live oak trees leads to the Visitor's Center and Museum, where there's a 15-minute film about life on the plantation. Walk from here to the ruins of Noble Jones's house, which was fortified against Indians, Spaniards and pirates. Nearby are the graves of Jones's wife, Sarah, and their youngest son, Inigo. The graves of Jones and other family members have been moved to Bonaventure Cemetery. Open Tues.-Sat., 9 a.m.-5 p.m.; Sun., 2-5:30 p.m. Admission.

DIRECTIONS: Leaving Wormsloe, turn left onto Skidaway and go to the first light; turn left on Ferguson Avenue for 2.1 miles to:

8. Bethesda Home for Boys — 9520 Ferguson Avenue, (912) 351-2040.

In 1738, the Rev. George Whitefield, Church of England minister to the Georgia colony, had a large "family" of children orphaned by yellow fever and other misfortunes. His eloquent pleas for money to build an orphanage touched many hearts and purses, including those of James Habersham, Benjamin Franklin, Lady Huntingdon, and others. In 1740, construction began at Bethesda (House of Mercy) Orphan Home, now the oldest orphanage in the country in continuous operation.

Bethesda began operation in 1742 on 650 lush acres of waterfront property on the Moon River. The original buildings, destroyed by fire in 1770, have been replaced by handsome brick buildings. The main building was built by the Union Society, which now operates Bethesda; Whitefield Chapel was given by the Colonial Dames; the outdoor theater came from the Trustees' Garden Club. There is also a carpentry shop, an Olympic-size swimming pool, a gymnasium and an auditorium, with stately oaks all around and the river nearby for boating, fishing, and crabbing. There's a museum with Bethesda memorabilia and a portrait of Lady Huntingdon.

Boys of school age live here in cottages with house parents and remain through high school. Through the Union Society and the Women's Board of Bethesda, funds are available for college. Many return with their fiancées to be married in Whitefield Chapel.

Grounds and chapel open daily 9 a.m.-5 p.m. Museum closed on weekends.

DIRECTIONS: Leaving Bethesda, turn left onto Ferguson Avenue and go to traffic light; turn left on Diamond Causeway for 2.9 miles to:

9. Skidaway Island State Park — (912) 598-2300.

Once the home of Robert and Dorothy Ripley Roebling and their children, Skidaway Island now has inviting public attractions, as well as The Landings, a protected residential community. Mrs. Roebling is one of "The Seven," to whom this book is dedicated.

The 506-acre campground has 88 tent and trailer sites, pool, picnic shelters, and restrooms with showers. The Sandpiper Nature Trail has identifying markers on trees and plants. The remains of a fort, once visited by Robert E. Lee, can be seen here. Of interest are displays of Indian culture, early settlers, and birds and animals indigenous to the area. $2 parking fee.

DIRECTIONS: Leaving the State Park, turn left onto Diamond Causeway; go through traffic light to STOP sign; turn left on McWhorter Drive for 4.3 miles to:

10. University of Georgia Marine Extension Services and Aquarium — 30 Ocean Science Circle; (912) 598-2496.

Get nose to nose with snapper, grouper, spadefish, flounder, loggerhead turtles, and other salt water wonders. One exhibit shows whale bones and bison teeth thought to be 25-30 million years old.

Hike the nature trail to see 'possums, raccoons, deer, and the lowly fiddler crab in the mud. Picnic tables overlook the Intracoastal Waterway. Hours: Weekdays 9 a.m.-4 p.m.; Sat. 12-5 p.m. Donation.

DIRECTIONS: Backtrack past Bethesda and through the light. Time for a map check. To return to your starting point the easiest way, though a bit longer, is Skidaway Road to Victory Drive (Highway 80) for 3.9 miles. After 5th light, look for signs to Islands Expressway and Historic District. Otherwise, plan your own return route and discover sights not included on this tour.

END OF TOUR

AREA DAY TRIPS

Bluffton, Hilton Head, and Beaufort, South Carolina

• **Bluffton**. (From Savannah, 25 miles)
DIRECTIONS: Cross the new Savannah River Bridge into South Carolina on Highway 17; turn right onto South Carolina 170, then right again onto South Carolina 46.

This small settlement on the May River is home to authors, artists and retired folks. Visit the Church of the Cross, a hauntingly lovely 1857 Episcopal church on the bend of the river, and Jacob Preston's pottery studio in an old church. There's a restaurant called the Squat and Gobble, plus an intriguing shop, Eggcentricities.

• **Hilton Head**. (From Savannah, 39 miles)
DIRECTIONS: From Bluffton, continue on Highway 46, then take Highway 278 onto Hilton Head Island.

Island life includes golf, boating, horseback riding, shopping, art galleries, concerts, and live theater in a setting of tidal marshes and sandy beaches.

• **Beaufort**. (From Savannah, 42 miles)
DIRECTIONS; From Hilton Head, drive north on Highway 278 for 27 miles; take Highway 170 north for 15 miles to Beaufort.

Uncrowded beaches, charter fishing, tennis, 6 golf courses, plus a delightful waterfront park are hallmarks of this winsome waterfront community. Handsome historic houses and St. Helena's Episcopal Church are must-sees here. Save time for the popular walking tour, telephone (803) 524-4330. Suggested side trips: Sheldon Church (1746), Parris Island Marine Base, Hunting Island State Park, The Penn Center on St. Helena's Island, and Lady's Island. The book and movie *The Prince of Tides*, were set here.

Golden Isles Getaway

Here's the route to Georgia's historic, beautiful Golden Isles, also known as barrier islands. Directions are for traveling south from Savannah on US 17 or I-95. (*Brown's I-95 Exit Guide* is a huge help.) Look for moss-draped oaks and picturesque plantation houses amid the mystical Marshes of Glynn.

• **Bryan County/Richmond Hill Welcome Center**, via US 17 or Exit 14 from I-95. Open 8:30 a.m.-5:30 p.m. Mon.-Sat., Sun. 1-5 p.m. (912) 756-2676.

• **Town of Richmond Hill and Richmond Hill Plantation**, via Georgia 144 or Exit 15 from I-95. Richmond Hill Plantation, on the banks of the Ogeechee River, was Henry Ford's winter home. Not open to the public. In the town of Richmond Hill is Ford Village, community buildings and residences built by Henry Ford (visitors welcome).

• **Fort McAllister**, via Georgia 144 or Exit 15 from I-95. Earthwork fortification on the south bank of the Ogeechee River. Withstood many attacks in the Civil War before falling to General William Tecumseh Sherman. Museum, gifts, admission. Open Tues.-Sat., 9 a.m.- 5 p.m. Sun., 2-5 p.m. closed Mon. (912) 727-2339 or (404) 656-3530.

• **Midway**, via Georgia 38 or Exit 13 from I-95. Quaint village midway between Savannah and Darien. Historic church and museum. Museum open Tues.-Sat. 10 a.m.-4 p.m.; Sun. 2-4 p.m.; closed Mon.; admission. Key to church available here. Nearby are the town of Sunbury and Fort Morris Historic Site. Also of interest:

•**Seabrook Village**, a glimpse into African-American life and architecture, c. 1900-1930. Open Tues.-Sat., 10 a.m.-5 p.m. Call (912) 884-7008 for more information.

• **Town of Darien and Fort King George Historic Site**, via Georgia 251 or Exit 10 from I-95. Living history presentation at Fort King George, England's southernmost American outpost in 1731-32. Admission.

• **Sapelo Island**, accessible only by ferryboat. Once home to Hudson Motor Company executive, Howard Coffin, and then tobacco magnate, R. J. Reynolds. Guided tours, admission.

• **Hofwyl-Broadfield Plantation**, via Georgia 99 or Exit 9 from I-95. Ante-bellum rice plantation, home of James Troup Dent and daughters, on banks of Altamaha River. Willed to Georgia by Miss Ophelia Dent. Visitor's Center, museum, guided tours of plantation house. Admission.

• **Golden Isles Parkway**, (Georgia 25) take Exit 8 from I-95. This coastal drive includes: the town of Brunswick, Jekyll Island, once winter sanctuary of wealthy industrialists whose "cottages" can still be seen; two-hour cruise available; hauntingly beautiful St. Simons Island with historic Christ Church, where Charles Wesley preached; ruins of Fort Frederica, built by Oglethorpe, magnificent Sea Island with famed resort and elegant "cottages."

• **Cumberland Island**, take Georgia 40 or Exit 2 from I-95 to St. Mary's. Reservations needed for 45-minute ferry boat ride on the *Cumberland Queen* to southernmost of Georgia's Golden Isles. Eighteen miles of undeveloped beaches, remains of the Carnegie family's estate, Dungeness. No shopping or transportation on island. National Park Service Rangers there to help. Camping for novices or experts.

• **Okefenokee Swamp National Wildlife Refuge**, via Okefenokee Parkway from Georgia 40 or Exit 2 from I-95. Enter through Okefenokee Swamp Park, eight miles south of Waycross. Programs, exhibits, wilderness walkways, boat tours, outdoor museum of pioneer life, in 700 square miles of a swamp that teems with plant and animal life. Seminole Indians named it Okefenokee, "Land of the Trembling Earth."

Arrange Golden Isles motorcoach tours from St. Simons Travelog, 113 Shore Rush Circle, (912) 638-5097, St. Simons Island, Ga.

Savannah National Wildlife Refuge

DIRECTIONS: From Savannah, take US 17-A across the new Savannah River Bridge; go 5 miles to the intersection of 17 and 17-A; go left on 17 for 2 miles to entrance at Laurel Hill Wildlife Drive. (912) 652-4415.

More than 250 species of birds can be seen flying free at Savannah National Wildlife Refuge, which covers over 26,000 acres of land and water. Peak bird-watching months are Nov.-Feb.

Drive slowly and you may see wood ducks, blue-winged teal, blue herons, and glossy ibis, as well as alligators and bobcats. Here are 25 miles of dikes for hiking and biking. (Get a map at the entrance.) Pets must be leashed. Remember—warm weather brings gnats and mosquitoes. Hours: Sunrise to sunset daily; no charge.

New Ebenezer

DIRECTIONS: From the Visitor's Center, go north on Martin Luther King, Jr., Boulevard; turn left (west) onto Bay Street; take 516 ramp into Garden City; follow Georgia 21 through Rincon and 3 miles more; take Highway 275 for 5 miles into Ebenezer. (27 miles from Visitor's Center.)

New Ebenezer (Stone of Help) was settled in 1736 by a rugged band of Lutherans from Salzburg, Austria, led in their search for religious freedom by Pastor John Martin Boltzius. Briefly the capital of Georgia, New Ebenezer was a bustling town with a plan of squares like that of Savannah. Legacies from New Ebenezer are Jerusalem Church (1769) and its grave-yard. Visit the Salzburger museum near the church. Industrious and cheerful, the Salzburgers produced silk and cotton and founded the country's first orphanage in 1738 (It closed 20 years later). The church has held regular services for more than 200 years. Museum hours: 3-5 p.m., Wed., Sat., and Sun.

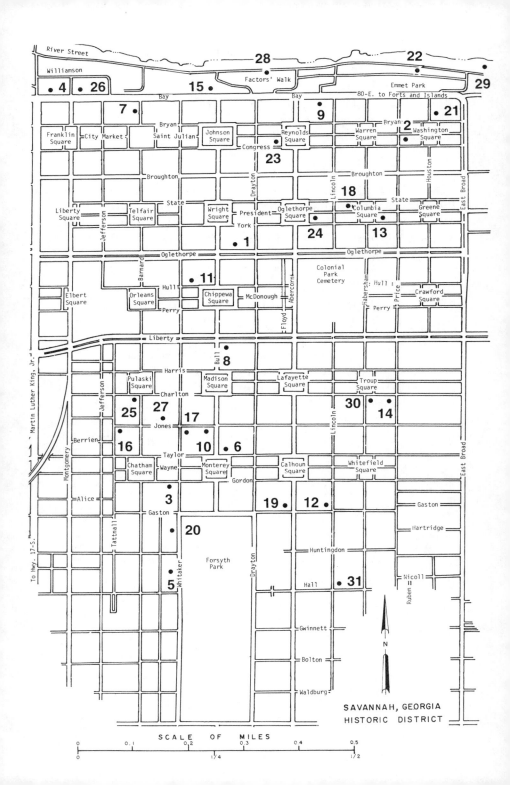

HOTELS, INNS AND HOSTELS

1. Ballastone Inn — 14 East Oglethorpe Avenue; 1-800-822-4553 or (912) 236-1484. Restored to ante-bellum elegance, designer fabrics, Scalamandre wallpaper, modern baths, full bar, front parlor, private garden. V, MC, AE.

2. B and B Inn — 501 East Saint Julian Street; (912) 236-9939. Two-story Victorian dwelling, family atmosphere, pets welcome, central location. V, MC, AE.

3. Bed and Breakfast Inn — 117 West Gordon Street at Chatham Square; (912) 238-0518. Amid stately mansions, restaurants, churches, antique shops. Sunny dining room, private garden. *Southern Living* and *Brown's Guide* give "thumbs up." V, MC, AE, D.

4. Best Western — 412 West Bay Street; 1-800-528-1234 or (912) 233-1011. Near City Market and River Street. Pool. No pets. V, MC, D, DC, AE.

5. Colophon — 609 Whitaker Street; (912) 233-2446. One spacious, non-smoking unit on Forsyth Park for up to four booklovers. Garden, off-street parking, Continental breakfast, TV, VCR, full kitchen.

6. Comer House — 2 East Taylor Street; (912) 234-2923. Two non-smoking suites on Monterey Square. Antiques, private parking, garden. Breakfast from stocked refrigerator.

7. Days Inn — 201 West Bay Street; 1-800-325-2525 or (912) 236-4440. Near River Street; 252 rooms and 57 suites, restaurant, free parking. V. MC, AE, D, DC. CB.

8. DeSoto Hilton — 15 East Liberty Street; 1-800-445-8667 or (912) 232-9000. Big hotel service and comfort, children and parking free. Outdoor pool, central location, concierge. V, MC, AE, D, DC, CB.

9. East Bay Inn — 225 East Bay Street; 1-800-500-1225 or (912) 238-1225. 28 rooms, restaurant, AAA/corporate rates. V, MC, AE, D, DC.

10. Eliza Thompson House — 5 West Jones Street; 1-800-348-9378 or (912) 236-3620. Federal-style home; 25 gracious rooms; breakfast and afternoon wine and cheese in parlor or garden. Great area for strolling. V, MC, AE.

11. Foley House — 14 West Hull Street; (912) 232-6622. On Chippewa Square; fireplaces, antiques, silver, china, oriental rugs. V, MC, AE.

12. Gastonian Inn — 220 East Gaston Street; 1-800-322-6603 or (912) 232-2869. 13 rooms and suites, antiques, fireplaces, Persian rugs, Charleston rice beds. Short walk to Forsyth Park and River Street. V, MC, AE.

13. Habersham at York Inn — 130 Habersham Street; (912) 234-2499. Enjoy a turn-of-the century interlude on Columbia Square; entrance garden. 48-hour free parking pass for historic district. V.

14. Hospitality House — 409 East Charlton Street; (912) 236-6448. Suite with fireplace, kitchen, Continental breakfast. Smoke free.

15. Hyatt Regency — 2 West Bay Street; 1-800-233-1234 or (912) 238-1234. Elevator down to River Street; "Windows" Restaurant overlooking river, spacious atrium, inside shops, concierge. V, MC, AE, DC, D, CB.

16. Jesse Mount House — 209 West Jones Street; (912) 236-1774. Four-story Savannah grey brick townhouse; furnishings from all over the world; fireplaces. V, MC, D.

17. Joan's on Jones — 17 West Jones Street; (912) 234-3863. Antiques, Continental breakfast, garden with fountain and southern plantings. Near Mrs. Wilkes' Restaurant.

18. Kehoe House — 123 Habersham Street; 1-800-820-1020 or (912) 232-1020. European-style inn on Columbia Square. Gourmet breakfast, afternoon tea and hors d'oeuvres. 15 rooms, entertainment area, courtyard. V, MC, AE, D.

19. Lion's Head Inn — 120 East Gaston Street; 1-800-355-LION or (912) 232-4580. Hospitality, comfort, and service in 19th century elegance. Smoke-free; walking distance to landmarks, shops, restaurants. V, MC, AE.

20. Magnolia Place Inn — 503 Whitaker Street; 1-800-238-7674 or (912) 236-7674. Grand inn overlooking Forsyth Park; great for walks, tennis, sunning. Conrad Aiken born here. Butterfly collection. V, MC, AE.

21. Mulberry Holiday Inn — 601 East Bay Street; 1-800-HOLIDAY or (912) 238-1200. Was cotton warehouse, stable, Coca-Cola bottling plant. Large fireplaces, afternoon tea in lounge, rooftop sauna, courtyard. V, MC, AE, D, DC.

22. Olde Harbour Inn — 508 East Factors' Walk; 1-800-553-6533 or (912) 234-4100. 24 suites overlooking Savannah River; elevator to River Street. V, MC, AE, DC, D, CB.

23. Planters' Inn — 29 Abercorn Street; (912) 232-5678. On Reynolds Square; easy walk to River Street and City Market. Near Pink House Restaurant. Credit cards: V, MC, AE, D.

24. Presidents' Quarters — 225 East President Street; 1-800-233-1776 or (912) 233-1600. 16 rooms and suites, fireplaces, afternoon tea, Continental breakfast, concierge, jacuzzi in garden. V, MC, AE, D.

25. Pulaski Square Inn — 203 West Charlton Street; 1-800-227-0650 or (912) 232-8055. Heart pine floors, antiques, oriental rugs. Walk to shops, restaurants, museums, churches, Civic Center. Carriage house ideal for families. V, MC, AE.

26. Quality Inn — 300 West Bay Street; 1-800-221-2222 or (912) 236-6321. Near River Street and City Market, restaurants. AAA/Senior discounts. V, MC, AE, DC, D.

27. Remshart-Brooks House — 106 West Jones Street; (912) 234-6928. Savannah grey brick dwelling dating from 1853; country antiques. One suite for up to 4 guests.

28. River Street Inn — 115 East River Street; 1-800-253-4229 or (912) 234-6400. Restored 1817 warehouse overlooking Savannah River. Four-poster, canopied beds; meeting rooms, secretary, business machines. V, AE, MC.

29. Savannah Marriott Riverfront — 100 General McIntosh Boulevard (east end of River Street) 1-800-333-3333 or (912) 233-7722. Two swimming pools, gymnasium, two restaurants, 8-story atrium, ballroom. V, MC, AE, D, DC.

30. Timmons House — 407 East Charlton Street; (912) 233-4456. One suite with sitting room, sleeps up to 4. Off-street parking; Continental breakfast.

31. Youth Hostel — 304 East Hall Street; (912) 236-7744. All ages; small fee; maximum stay 3 nights. Sheets provided, bring towels. TV room, kitchens, bunk beds. Closed 10:30 a.m.-5 p.m. for cleaning.

Reservation Services—Savannah

• **RSVP Reservation Service** — 1-800-729-7787 or (912) 232-7787. For historic district.

• **Savannah Historic Inns and Guest Houses** — 1-800-262-4667 or (912) 233-7666. For historic district.

• **Savannah Tourist Guide** — 1-800-791-9393 or (912) 355-1740. For Savannah and Savannah Beach.

At Savannah Beach (Tybee)

• **Best Western Dunes Inn** — 1409 Butler Avenue; 1-800-528-1234 or (912) 786-4591. One block from beach; pool, kitchenettes, suites, jacuzzi. V, MC, AE, DC, D.

• **Cobb's Motel and Apartments** — 17th Street and oceanfront; (912) 786-4772. Comfortable, older buildings with picnic tables, grills. No pets.

• **Days Inn** — 1402 Butler Avenue; 1-800-325-2525 or (912) 786-4576. One block from ocean, near restaurants; pool. Days Inn chain started here, V, MC, AE, D, DC, CB.

• **DeSoto Beach Motel** — 212 Butler Avenue; (912) 786-4542. Let surf sounds sing you to sleep in this modernized, 1938 hotel. Tiki bar, entertainment Wed.-Sun. V, MC, AE.

• **EconoLodge Tybee** — 404 Butler Avenue; 1-800-446-6900 or (912) 786-4535. Oceanside with Tiki Bar, pool; near tennis, volleyball. V, MC, AE, DC, D.

• **Hunter House** — 1701 Butler Avenue; (912) 786-7515. Spacious beach house with large upstairs porch; one block from ocean; fine dining at night. V, MC, AE.

• **Lighthouse Point Condo Rentals** — 203 First Street; 1-800-755-8562 or (912) 786-5913. Ocean views, tennis, pools. V, MC, AE, DC, D.

• **Ocean Plaza Inn** — 15th Street and oceanfront; (912) 786-7664. Two hundred yards from dunes and beach; two pools. V, MC, AE, DC, D.

• **Savannah Beach and Racquet Club** — 1217 Bay Street; 1-800-476-0807 or (912) 786-4364. Condominiums with balconies overlooking ocean; tennis, pool. V, MC, AE, D, DC.

• **Tybrisa Beach Resorts** — One 15th Street; 1-800-868-4080 or (912) 786-4080. Condominiums near beach; pool, tennis, shuffleboard. V, MC, AE.

Reservation Service—Savannah Beach

• **Tybee Beach Rentals** — (912) 786-8805 or 1-800-755-8562. Daily, weekly, monthly rentals for cottages, villas, and condominiums. V, MC, AE.

Credit Cards:
V — Visa
AE — American Express
DC — Diners Club
D — Discover
MC — Master Card
CB — Carte Blanche
WCA — Wheel chair accessible

RESTAURANTS AND NIGHT LIFE

• **Bayou Café** — River Street at Abercorn ramp; (912) 233-6411. Blues nightly; Cajun cooking. Daily, 11 a.m.-3 a.m. DC, V, D, MC, CB.

• **Bistro** — 309 West Congress Street; (912) 233-6266. Art gallery café; southern coastal cuisine. Sun.-Thurs., 6-10:30 p.m.; Fri.-Sat., 6 p.m.-12 a.m. V, MC, AE.

• **Boar's Head** — River Street at Lincoln Street ramp; (912) 232-3196. 19th century cotton warehouse; "she crab" soup, boiled shrimp, catfish fillet, bouillabaisse. Lunch: Tues.-Fri., 11:30 a.m.-3 p.m.; Sat.-Sun., 11:30 a.m.-4 p.m. Dinner: Tues.-Sun., 5:30 p.m.-late. V, MC, AE.

• **Bottom Line** — 206 West Saint Julian Street; (912) 232-0812. Live music, dance floor. Tues.-Thurs., 7:30 p.m.-1 a.m., Fri.-Sat., 7:30 p.m.-2 a.m. V, D, MC, AE.

• **Broughton Street Firehouse** — 420 East Broughton Street; (912) 233-1353. Varied menu with rooms for elegant or casual dining, game room, lounge. Mon.-Thurs., 10:30 a.m.-2 a.m.; Fri.-Sat., 10:30 a.m.-3 a.m. V, MC, AE, CB.

• **Café Chutzpah** — 251 Bull Street; (912) 234-5007. Mediterranean bistro; French, Italian, Moroccan, Greek, Spanish dishes; adjoining "wearable art" boutique. Boutique: Mon.-Sat., 10 a.m.-5:30 p.m.; café: 11:30 a.m.-3 p.m. V, MC.

• **Chao Chinese** — 152 Montgomery Street, at corner of Oglethorpe; (912) 231-8891. Hunan, Szechuan and American dishes to eat in or take out. Catering, lunch buffet, free delivery with $10 order. Mon.–Thurs., 11:30 a.m.–9:30 p.m.; Fri., 11:30 a.m.–10:30 p.m.; Sat., noon–10:30 p.m.; Sun., noon–9:30 p.m. V, MC, AE, D, DC. WCA.

• **Chart House** — 202 West Bay Street; (912) 234-6686. Ships' chandlery/cotton warehouse; outside decks for views of Savannah River; steaks, prime rib, seafood. Sun.-Thurs., 5-10 p.m.; Fri.-Sat., 5-11 p.m. V, MC, AE, D, DC, CB. WCA on first floor.

• **City Market Café** — 224 West Saint Julian Street; (912) 236-7133. Indoor/outdoor dining; unusual beers; seafood; pasta. Lunch: Mon.-Fri., 11 a.m.-3:30 p.m.; Sat.-Sun., 11 a.m.-3 p.m. Dinner: 6-9 p.m. daily. MC, V, AE, D, DC. WCA.

• **Clary's** — 404 Abercorn Street; (912) 233-0402. Friendly café in converted drugstore; salads, burgers, homemade soups. Mon.-Fri., 6:30 a.m.-4 p.m.; Sat., 8 a.m.-1 p.m.; Sun., 9 a.m.-2 p.m. V, MC, AE, DC, D.

• **Crossroads** — 219 West Saint Julian Street; (912) 234-5438. Live music and dancing. Mon.-Sat., 5 p.m.-3 a.m. V, MC, AE.

• **Crystal Beer Parlor** — 301 West Jones Street; (912) 232-1153. Family oriented; legendary burgers, soups, French fries with skin on. Mon.-Sat., 11 a.m.-9 p.m. AE, D, V, MC. WCA via parking lot entrance.

• **Dockside** — 201 West River Street; (912) 236-9253. Indoor/outdoor dining in 1792 ships' chandlery, said to be oldest masonry building in Georgia. Tues.-Sun., 11:30 a.m.-9 p.m. V, MC, AE, D, DC.

• **Elizabeth on 37th Street** — 105 East 37th Street; (912) 236-5547. Outstanding regional cooking in a southern mansion; *Food* *and Wine* magazine hails this as one of the top 25 restaurants in the country. Mon.-Sat., 6-10 p.m. V, MC, AE.

• **Exchange Tavern** — 201 East River Street; (912) 232-7088. Local seafood, char-grilled steaks, "Oompah's" famous sour cream potato salad. Mon.-Sat., 11 a.m.-2 a.m.; Sun., 11 a.m.-midnight. V, MC, AE, DC, CB, D.

• **F. C. Goodfellows'** — 115 East River Street; (912) 233-5288. Entertainment nightly; great burgers, prime rib, seafood. Mon.-Sat., 11 a.m.-late; Sun., 12:30 p.m.-late. V, MC, D.

• **Fiddler's** — 2909 River Drive; Thunderbolt, (912) 354-8409. Fresh seafood and steaks on the banks of the Wilmington River. Tues.-Sun., 11:30 a.m.-10:30 p.m. V, MC, D.

• **45 South** — 20 East Broad Street; (912) 233-1881. Elegant dining; fine wine cellar; venison in port wine, poached oysters, backfin crabmeat. Coat and tie. Mon.-Thurs., 6-9 p.m.; Fri.-Sat., 6-9:30 p.m. V, MC, AE, DC.

• **Gallery Espresso Café** — 3 East Liberty Street; (912) 233-5348. The pinnacle of coffee experience plus cakes and pastries; across from DeSoto Hotel. Mon.-Thurs., 8:30 a.m.-2:30 a.m.; Fri.-Sun., 8:30 a.m.-3 a.m.

• **Garibaldi's** — 315 West Congress Street; (912) 232-7118. Italian cuisine acclaimed in *Gourmet* magazine; seafood, veal, Chocolate Oblivion dessert. Sun.-Thurs., 6-10:30 pm; Fri.-Sat., 5:30 p.m.-midnight. V, MC, AE. WCA.

• **Grapevine** — 115 East River Street; (912) 238-8004. Authentically Italian; seafood buffet on weekends. Balcony overlooking Savannah River. Mon.-Fri., 7 a.m.-10 p.m.; Sat.-Sun., 8 a.m.-11 p.m. V, MC, D.

• **Hannah's East** — 20 East Broad Street, atop the Pirates' House; (912) 233-2225. Live music with Ben Tucker, Emma Kelly and friends. Hors d'oeuvres, appetizer menu. Mon., 5-9 p.m.; Tues.-Wed., 5-ll p.m.; Thurs., 5 p.m.-midnight; Fri.-Sat., 5 p.m.-1 a.m. V, MC, AE, D, CB, DC.

• **Huey's** — 115 East River Street; (912) 234-7385. Cajun dishes; ideal for "people watching"; live jazz on weekends. Mon.-Thurs., 8 a.m.-10 p.m.; Fri.-Sat., 8 a.m.-11 p.m.; Sun., 8 a.m.-10 p.m. V, MC, AE, D. WCA.

• **Il Pasticcio** — 2 East Broughton Street; (912) 231-8888. Festive Italian restaurant, bakery, and take-out counter; woodburning pizza oven and rotisserie; espresso bar. Take-outs daily from 11:30 a.m. Lunch, Tues.-Sun., 11:30 a.m.-2:30 p.m.; Dinner, Tues.-Thurs. and Sun., 6-10 p.m.; Fri.-Sat., 6-11 p.m. V, MC, AE, D. WCA.

• **Jean Louise** — 321 Jefferson Street; (912) 234-3211. Intimate and elegant in a restored 1890 tavern. Lunch, Mon.-Fri., 11:30 a.m.-2 p.m. Dinner, Mon.-Sat., 5-10 p.m. Reservations suggested. V, MC, AE. WCA.

• **John and Linda's** — 303 West Saint Julian Street; (912) 233-2626. Bustling restaurant in City Market area; happy hour 4-7 p.m.; specialties include grouper, oysters, shrimp, and scallops. Lunch, Mon.-Fri., ll:30 a.m.-2:30 p.m.; Dinner, Sun.-Thurs., 6-10 p.m., Fri.-Sat. 6-11 p.m. MC, V, AE.

• **Johnny Harris** — 1651 East Victory Drive; (912) 354-7810. Famous for barbecue; sauce sold all over the country. Mon.-Thurs., ll:30 a.m.-10:30 p.m.; Fri., ll:30 a.m.-midnight; Sat., 11:30 a.m.-12:30 a.m. V, MC, AE, D. WCA.

• **Juicy Lucy's** — 241 Abercorn Street; (912) 231-1707. Breakfast and lunch, plus deli take-outs, catering, celebrity chefs. South American decor to admire and/or purchase. Daily from 8 a.m.-after lunch. WCA.

• **Kevin Barry's** — 117 West River Street; (912) 233-9626. Irish pub with handsome well-stocked bar, Irish food and music. Mon.-Fri., 4 p.m.-3 a.m.; Sat., 11 a.m.-3 a.m.; Sun., 12:30 p.m.-2 a.m. V, MC, AE, D.

• **McDonough's Pub** — 21 East McDonough Street; (912) 233-6136. Down home southern cooking. Daily from 11:00 a.m.-3 a.m. AE.

• **Malone's** — 27 Barnard Street; (912) 234-3059. Bar and grill with dance floor; live music in courtyard on weekends. Large screen TV; gameroom. Mon.-Thurs., 11 a.m.-midnight; Fri.-Sun., 11 a.m.-2 a.m. V, MC, AE, DC, CB.

• **Mulberry Holiday Inn** — 601 East Bay Street; (912) 238-1200. Breakfast/lunch buffet, evenings a la carte. Gracious and friendly. Daily: 6:30-10 a.m.; 11 a.m.-2 p.m.; 6-10 p.m. V, MC, AE, DC, D.

• **Olympia Café** — 5 East River Street; (912) 233-3131. Authentic Greek cuisine; take-out deli. Ice cream and fat-free yogurt in 32 flavors. Mon.-Sun., 11 a.m.-11 p.m. V, MC, AE, D.

• **Palmer's Seafood House** — 80 Wilmington Island Road; (912) 897-2611. Fifteen minutes from historic district; family restaurant with seafood galore; outdoor deck on Turner's Creek. Mon., 5-10 p.m.; Tues.-Sat., 11 a.m.-10 p.m.; Sun., 11 a.m.-9 p.m. V, MC, AE, DC, D.

• **Pavilion Restaurant** — in DeSoto Hotel, 15 East Liberty Street; (912) 232-9000. Relaxed atmosphere, southern cooking with buffet. Breakfast: Mon.-Fri., 6:30-10 a.m.; Sat., 6:30-11 a.m.; Sun., 7 a.m.-10 a.m. Lunch: daily (except Sat.) 11:00 a.m.-2 p.m. Dinner: Tues.-Sat., 6-10 p.m. MC, V, AE, DC. WCA.

• **Pink House Restaurant and Tavern** — 23 Abercorn Street; (912) 232-4286. Historic house with southern cuisine, heart-smart cooking. Daily: restaurant, 6-10:30 p.m.; tavern, 1:30 p.m.-

2 a.m. V, MC, AE.

• **Pinkie Masters' Lounge** — 318 Drayton Street; (912) 238-0447. Favorite political hangout; Jimmy Carter and Al Gore stood on bar and made speeches. Mon.-Sat., 4 p.m.-3 a.m.

• **Pirates' House** — 20 East Broad Street; (912) 233-5757. Once a pirate pub, now a family restaurant with 15 rooms. Wide variety of southern favorites. Lunch: Mon.-Sun., 11:30 a.m.-2:30 p.m. Dinner: 5:30-9 p.m. V, MC, AE, DC, CB, D. WCA.

• **Riverhouse Seafood** — 125 West River Street; (912) 234-1900. Riverside view of tugs and freighters; sirloin, lobster, hickory chicken, seafood. Mon.-Thurs., 11 a.m.-10 p.m.; Fri.-Sat., 11 a.m.-11 p.m. V, MC, AE, CB, DC.

• **River's Edge** — in Savannah Marriott Riverfront Hotel, 100 General McIntosh Boulevard; (912) 233-7722. Buffet (healthy start, continental, hefty); omelette and waffle stations. Daily, 6:30 a.m.- 11 p.m. V, MC, AE, D, DC.

• **River's End** — River Drive, Thunderbolt; (912) 354-2973. View of quaint fishing village; seafood, steaks, Cornish hens, duck, veal, and lamb. Mon.-Thurs., 5-10 p.m.; Fri.-Sat., 5-11 p.m. V, MC, AE, DC, D. WCA.

• **Sam Fink's Delicatessen** — 11 West Liberty Street; (912) 236-3354. Creative sandwiches and salads; 110 varieties of bottled and draught beer. Mon.-Thurs., 11 a.m.-10 p.m., Fri.-Sat., 11 a.m.-12 a.m.; Sun., 11 a.m.-9 p.m. V, MC, AE. WCA.

• **17 hundred 90 Inn Restaurant and Lounge** — 307 East President Street; (912) 236-7122. Favorite of locals. Rack of lamb, flounder, salmon. Lunch: Mon.-Fri., 12-2 p.m. Dinner daily, 6-10 p.m. V, MC, AE.

• **Shrimp Factory** — 313 East River Street; (912) 236-4229. Lobster, soft shell/deviled crabs, chops, pine bark stew, gumbo;

churned ice cream. Mon.-Thurs., 11 a.m.-10 p.m.; Fri.-Sat., 11 a.m.-11 p.m. V, MC, AE, CB, D.

• **Shucker's Restaurant and Oyster Bar** — 225 West River Street; (912) 236-1427. Hatch-cover tables; fresh seafood; children's menu. Sun.-Thurs., 11:30 a.m.-10:30 p.m.; Fri., 11:30 a.m.-11 p.m.; Sat., 11:30 a.m.-midnight. V, MC. AE, D.

• **606 East Café** — 319 West Congress Street; (912) 236-5113. Whimsical decor; courtyard; food's great, too! Visit the WC even if it's just to enjoy the artwork. Sun.-Wed., 11 a.m.-10 p.m.; Thurs.-Sat., 11 a.m.-11 p.m. V, MC, AE. WCA.

• **Six Pence Pub** — 245 Bull Street; (912) 233-3151. Friendly folks; plowman's lunch; European beers. Mon.-Thurs., 11:30 a.m.-midnight; Fri.-Sat., 11:30 a.m.-1 a.m.; Sun., 12:30-10 p.m. D, MC, V, AE.

• **Skyler's** — 225 East Bay Street; (912) 232-3995. Basement of historic inn; Vietnamese/American cuisine. Lunch: Mon.-Fri., 11 a.m.-3 p.m. Dinner: Wed.-Thurs., 6-9 p.m.; Fri.-Sat., 6-10 p.m. V, MC, AE. WCA.

• **Snapper's** — Highway 80 and Bryan Woods Road; (912) 897-6101. Casual marsh view setting, 10 minutes from historic district. Family fare including seafood, chicken, steaks. Children's menu. Mon.-Sat., 11 a.m.-10 p.m.; Sun., 11 a.m.-9 p.m. MC, V, AE. WCA.

• **Spanky's** — 317 East River Street; (912) 236-3009. Pizza, burgers, chicken fingers, fried shrimp in a casual setting. Daily, 11:30 a.m.-late. V, MC, AE.

• **Teeple's** — 2917 River Drive in Thunderbolt; (912) 354-1157. Ten minutes from historic district; pick shrimp/crabs, pry oysters, clams. Daily 11 a.m.-10 p.m. V, MC, AE.

• **The Taj** — 110 West Congress Street; (912) 231-9815. Indian cuisine, decor, staff. Lunch: ll:30 a.m.-3 p.m. Dinner: 5-10 p.m. AE.

• **Times on Bay** — 9 East Bay Street; (912) 232-5116. 1853 bank building; English club atmosphere; French-inspired cuisine. Dress code. Tues.-Sun., 5-10 p.m. V, MC, D, AE. WCA.

• **Troup Square Café** — 321 Habersham Street; (912) 231-8037. Home cooking in a relaxed setting; omelettes from 'round the world. Mon.-Fri., breakfast at 7 a.m., lunch 11 a.m.-2 p.m. Sat.-Sun. brunch, 8 a.m.-2 p.m.

• **Velvet Elvis** — 127 East Congress Street; (912) 236-0665. Alternative music; retro-70s flavor. Mon.-Sat., 8 p.m.-3 a.m. with live bands on Fri. and Sat. Beer only.

• **Vinnie-Van-Go-Go's** — 317 West Bryan Street; (912) 233-6394. Manhole-cover-sized pizza, salads; bike deliveries. Mon.-Thurs., 4-11:30 p.m.; Fri.-Sat., noon-2 a.m.; Sun., noon-11:30 p.m.

• **White Horse Restaurant and Saloon** — 9 Drayton Street; (912) 232-8501. Massive bar brought from Grand Central Station in the 1800s; famous steer-burgers on sourdough buns. Mon.-Sat. 11 a.m.-midnight; Sun., ll:30 a.m.-midnight. AE, V, MC, DC, D.

• **Williams' Seafood Restaurant** — 8010 Tybee Road; (912) 897-2219. Nothing fancy here, just lots of good seafood. A Savannah favorite. Mon.-Sat., 11:30 a.m.-9:30 p.m.; Sun., 11 a.m.-9 p.m. V, MC, AE, D. WCA.

• **Windows** — 2 West Bay in Hyatt Hotel; (912) 238-1234. Panoramic view of new Savannah River bridge; weekday buffet; hearty Sun. country breakfast buffet. Sun.-Thurs., 6:30 a.m.-10 p.m.; Fri.-Sat., 6:30 a.m.-11 p.m. V, MC, AE, DC, CB. WCA.

At Savannah Beach (Tybee)

• **Breakers** — 212 Butler Avenue in DeSoto Beach Motel; (912) 786-6658. Wed.-Sun., 7:30-11:30 a.m. and 5-10 p.m. V, MC, AE.

• **Breakfast Club** — 1500 Butler Avenue; (912) 786-5984. A favorite with Tybeenians; bikinis and flipflops welcome. Daily, 6 a.m.-1 p.m. V, MC.

• **Cap'n Chris** — 1415 Butler Avenue; (912) 786-4516. Seafood and country cookin' buffet Fri. and Sat. nights; breakfast buffet on Sat. and Sun. Daily 6:30 a.m.-11 p.m. V, MC.

• **Crab Shack at Chimney Creek** — off Highway 80 on Tybee Island; (912) 786-9857. Near the water, indoors or outdoors; crab cakes are a specialty. Daily, 11:30 a.m.-10 p.m. V, MC.

• **Fannie's on the Beach** — 1613 Strand (near 17th Street); (912) 786-6109. Gourmet pizza; appetizers galore; children's menu. Winter: Wed.–Fri. 4 p.m.–late (closed Mon.–Tues.), Sat.–Sun., noon–late. Summer: daily, 10 a.m.–late. WCA.

• **Hunter House** — 1701 Butler Avenue; (912) 786-7515. The pot roast dinner is memorable. May-Sept.: Mon.-Thurs., 6-9 p.m.; Fri.-Sun., 6-10 p.m. (Closed Mon. the rest of year.) V, MC, AE.

• **MacElwee's Seafood** — North End of Butler Avenue; (912) 786-4259. Grilled and blackened fish, Black Angus beef; children's menu. Mon.-Fri., 2-11 p.m.; Sat.-Sun., 11:30 a.m.-11 p.m. V, MC, DC, D, AE.

• **Mar Lin Marina on Tybee–Sunset Bar and Grill** — 14th Street and Back River; (912) 786-7508. Watch sunsets and dolphins from outside deck. Wed. and Fri. night seafood specials; Sun. brunch. V, MC, AE, D. WCA.

• **The Oar House** — 1311 Butler Avenue; (912) 786-5055. Nautical decor, ceiling fans; seafood in a salt air setting. V, MC, AE, DC, D. WCA.

• **Spanky's Beachside** — 404 Butler Avenue; (912) 786-5520. Feast on family fare, then walk on the beach. Sun.-Thurs., 11 a.m.-11 p.m.; Sat.-Sun., 11 a.m.-midnight. V, MC, AE.

SHOPPING

• **Antique Alley** — 121 East Gwinnett Street; (912) 236-6281. Estate items, paintings, porcelain, glass. Open Mon.-Sat., 9 a.m.-5 p.m., or by appointment.

• **Arts and Crafts Emporium** — 234 Bull Street; (912) 238-0003. Local and national displays of prints, jewelry, textiles, pottery, glass, paintings. Open Mon.-Sat., 10 a.m.-6 p.m.; Sun., noon-5 p.m.

• **Blatner's** — 347 Abercorn Street; (912) 234-1210. Military items, guns, folk art, bottles, baseball cards. Open Mon., Wed., Sat., 10 a.m.-4 p.m.; Tues., Thurs., Fri., 11:30 a.m.-5:30 p.m.; Sun., 3:30-5:30 p.m.

• **Book Lady** — 17 West York Street; (912) 233-3628. Used/rare books, search service. Open Mon.-Fri., 10 a.m.-5 p.m.; Sat., 10 a.m.-2 p.m.

• **Bull Street Gallery** — 248 Bull Street; (912) 233-4307. Pottery, glasswork, jewelry, sculpture by local artists. Open daily, 10 a.m.-6 p.m.; closed Tues. and Sun.

• **Carriage House Antiques and Designs** — 135 Bull Street; (912) 233-5405. Porcelain, bronze, cut glass, silver. Open Mon.-Sat., 10 a.m.-5 p.m.

• **Charlotte's Corner** — 1 West Liberty Street; (912) 233-8061.

Remembrances of Savannah — children's clothing. Open Mon.-Sat., 10 a.m.-6 p.m.

• **Checkered Moon** — 422 Whitaker Street; (912) 233-5132. Painted furniture and other functional art, local pottery, handmade jewelry. Open Mon.-Sat. (closed Tues.), 10 a.m.-6 p.m.; Sun., 11 a.m.-3 p.m.

• **Bob Christian** — 12 West Harris Street; (912) 234-6866. Original decorative arts for the home. Open Mon.-Fri., 10 a.m.-3 p.m.

• **Cobb Galleries** — 417 Whitaker Street; (912) 234-1582. Coins, steins, Depression glass, Wedgwood china, cow creamers. Open Mon.-Fri., 10 a.m.-5 p.m.; Sat., 10 a.m.-4 p.m.

• **Compass Prints** — 205 West Congress Street; (912) 234-3537. Paintings, prints, and bronzes by Ray Ellis. Open Mon.-Fri., 10 a.m.-4 p.m.; Sat., 11 a.m.-3 p.m.

• **Cottage Shop** — 2422 Abercorn Street; (912) 233-3820. China, crystal, lamps, custom bed covers, linens. Open Mon.-Fri., 9:30 a.m.-5:30 p.m.

• **Creative Collectibles** — 129 East Liberty Street; (912) 238-9148. Local artists and crafters; baskets, dolls, bird houses, and woodcraft. Open Mon.-Sat., 10 a.m.-6 p.m.

• **D and B Collection** — 408 Bull Street; (912) 238-0087. A captivating browse of decorative art; lamps, mirrors, silver, clay, and brass. Open Mon.-Sat., 10 a.m.-6 p.m.; Sun., 2-6 p.m.

• **Davenport House Museum Shop** — Habersham Street entrance of 324 East State Street; (912) 236-8097. Unique Savannah items. Open daily. 10 a.m.-4 p.m.

• **Michael DeCook Antiques** — 20 West Hull Street; (912) 232-7149. Climb one flight of stairs for traditional furniture and garden ornaments. Open Mon.-Sat., 10 a.m.-4 p.m.

• **DeLoach Antiques and Garden Shop** — 12 West Jones Street; (912) 238-1387. Neo-classical English and French furniture, gifts, decorative pieces. Open Mon.-Sat., 10 a.m.-5 p.m.

• **Dreamweaver** — 306 West Saint Julian Street; (912) 236-9003. Books, tapes, gifts for personal growth, herbs. Open Mon.-Sat., 10 a.m.-6 p.m.; Sun., noon-5 p.m.

• **V. and J. Duncan Antique Maps and Prints** — 12 East Taylor Street; (912) 232-0338. Americana, books, and fine, decorative maps and prints. Open Mon.-Sat., 10 a.m.-5 p.m.

• **Eclectic Relics** — 345 Abercorn Street; (912) 232-4874. Victorian to art deco, faux finishes, vintage clothing. Open Mon.-Sat., 10 a.m.-5 p.m.; Sun., 1-5 p.m.

• **Enchantments** — 311 Bull Street on Madison Square; (912) 231-9323. Dolls and stuffed animals by Steiff, Ty, and R. John Wright for collections or play. Open Mon.-Sat., 10 a.m.-5 p.m., or by appointment.

• **English Accent** — 509 Lincoln Street; (912) 233-9589. Carriage house with boxes, furniture, and unique accessories. Open Mon.-Sat. (closed Wed.), 11 a.m.-5 p.m.

• **Exhibit A Gallery of Savannah College of Art and Design** — 342 Bull Street; (912) 238-2480. Photographs, lithographs, paintings, weaving by SCAD students. Displays change regularly. Open Mon.-Fri., 9 a.m.-5 p.m.; Sat., 10 a.m.-4 p.m.

• **Gallery 209** — 209 East River Street; (912) 236-4583. Co-op of 30 artists on two floors of cotton warehouse. Open Mon.-Sat., 10:30 a.m.-5:30 p.m.; Sun., noon-5:30 p.m.

• **Gaucho's** — 250 Bull Street at Liberty; (912) 232-7414. Unique clothing, accessories, jewelry and gifts from Mexico, Indonesia, and other countries. Open Mon.-Sat., 10 a.m.-6 p.m.

• **International Oasis Gallery** — above Il Pasticcio Restaurant, Bull and Broughton Streets; (912) 236-4736. A changing collection of contemporary and traditional painting and sculpture, national and international; many media and styles; frames and custom framing. Open Tues.-Sat., 10 a.m.-4 p.m.

• **Japonica** — 13 West Charlton Street; (912) 236-1613. Antiques and unusual gifts; decor consultation. Open Mon.-Sat., 10 a.m.-5 p.m.

• **Jere's** — 9 North Jefferson Street; (912) 236-2815. Thirty thousand foot showroom with European furniture, pianos, and pub bars. Open Mon.-Sat., 9:30 a.m.-5 p.m.

• **Little House** — 107 East Gordon Street; (912) 232-1551. Distinctive gifts since 1922. Open Mon.-Fri., 10 a.m.-6 p.m.; Sat., 10 a.m.-5 p.m.

• **Littlejohn's, Ltd.** — 101 West Jones Street; (912) 233-8367. Lamps, tassels, porcelains, bell pulls, pillows, finials, brass. Open Mon.-Fri., 11 a.m.-6 p.m.; Sat., 11 a.m.-5 p.m.

• **Francis McNairy Antiques** — 411 Abercorn Street; (912) 232-6411. Early 19th century American and European furniture, medieval to 1950s. Open Monday-Saturday, 10 a.m.-4 p.m., or by appointment.

• **Memory Lane Antiques Mall** — 230 West Bay Street; (912) 232-0975. Eight thousand square feet of glassware, furniture, and collectibles. Open Mon.-Sat., 10 a.m.-5 p.m.

• **Mulberry Tree** — 17 West Charlton Street; (912) 236-4656. Treasures old and new, including quilts, dolls, baskets, Savannah boxes, bird houses. Open Mon.-Sat., 10 a.m.-5 p.m.

• **Pinch of the Past** — 232 West Broughton Street; (912) 232-

5563. Architectural antiques, hardware; estate contents, brass polishing, restoration. Open Mon.-Sat., 9 a.m.-5 p.m.

• **Profiles Accessories** — 307 Bull Street; (912) 233-3892. Near DeSoto Hilton; unique high fashion jewelry, belts, handbags. Open Mon.-Sat., 10 a.m.-5:30 p.m.

• **Alex Raskin, Antiques** — 441 Bull Street; (912) 232-8205. Unusual decorative antique furniture, paintings, oriental rugs. Open Mon.-Sat., 10 a.m.-5 p.m.

• **Regina's Books and Cards** — 4947 Waters Avenue; (912) 353-7447. Full service bookstore with large regional and lifestyles sections. Open Mon.-Fri., 10 a.m.-6 p.m.; Sat., 10 a.m.-5:30 p.m.

• **Riverworks Craft Gallery** — 105 East River Street; (912) 236-2012. Fine crafts and gifts by many artists. Open Mon.-Sat., 10 a.m.-6 p.m.; Sun., 11 a.m.-7 p.m.

• **Saints and Shamrocks** — 309 Bull Street; (912) 233-8858. Irish imports, hats, sweaters, pottery. Religious statues, rosaries. Open Mon.-Sat., 9 a.m.-5:30 p.m.

• **Savannah Art Association** — Bishop's Court, Trustees' Garden; (912) 232-7731. Paintings, sculpture by local artists. 5-6 shows yearly. Open Mon.-Fri., 11 a.m.-5 p.m.; Sat.-Sun., 1-4 p.m.

• **Savannah Galleries** — 30 East Bryan Street; (912) 232-1234. 18th and 19th century American, English and French furniture. Rugs, clocks, copper. Open Tues.-Fri. 10 a.m.-5 p.m.; Sat. 10 a.m.-4 p.m.

• **School of Visual Arts/Savannah, Lower Level Gallery** — 110 East President Street; (912) 651-1280. Exhibitions of work by students and faculty. Mon.–Fri., 9 a.m.–5 p.m., Sat., 1–4 p.m.

• **Scrooge and Marley Antiques** — 137 Bull Street; (912) 236-9099. American, English, French silver, jewelry, paintings, prints. Open Mon.-Sat., 10 a.m.-5 p.m.; Sun., 11 a.m.-2 p.m.

• **Shaver, E., Booksellers** — 326 Bull Street, behind DeSoto Hilton; (912) 234-7257. 12 rooms of hardbacks and paperbacks, rare books and maps, search service. Open Mon.-Sat., 9 a.m.-6 p.m.

• **Sign of the Clef** — 307 West Bryan Street; (912) 234-1178. Musical gifts, learning games, chimes, note cards. Open Mon.-Sat., 10 a.m.-6 p.m.; Sun., 10:30 a.m.-2 p.m.

• **Signature Gallery** — 303 West Saint Julian Street; (912) 233-3082. Paintings, glass, clay, jewelry by local artists. Open Mon.-Sat., 10 a.m.-5 p.m.; Sun., noon-5 p.m.

• **Simply Silver** — 14-A Bishop's Court, Trustees' Garden; (912) 238-3652. Sterling flatware in active and inactive patterns. Open Mon.-Sat., 10 a.m.-5:30 p.m.

• **Small Pleasures** — 15 East Harris Street; (912) 236-0111. Old and new gifts and mementos, tokens of friendship. Open Mon.-Sat., 10 a.m.-5 p.m.

• **Arthur Smith, Antiques** — 1 West Jones Street; (912) 236-9701. American and European furniture, Chinese porcelains. Appraisals, estate sales. Open Mon.-Fri., 9:30 a.m.–4:30 p.m.; Sat., 10 a.m.–4 p.m.

• **Southern Antiques and Interiors** — 28 Abercorn Street on Reynolds Square; (912) 236-5080. English, American and continental furniture, fireplace accessories, and oriental rugs. Open Mon.-Sat., 10 a.m.–5 p.m.

• **Taylor House** — 10 West Taylor Street; (912) 234-5520. Armani porcelains, old and new Limoges china, Wedgwood and Nippon china, original etchings. Mon.–Sat., 10 a.m.–5 p.m.; Sun., noon–3 p.m.

• **John Tucker, Fine Arts** — 5 West Charlton Street; (912) 231-8161. Paintings by established artists, 1650-1984. Open Mon.-Sat., 10 a.m.-6 p.m.

• **Claire West Antiques and Fine Linen** — 413 Whitaker Street; (912) 236-8163. Imported linens, period antiques. Open Mon.-Sat., 10 a.m.-5 p.m.

• **Wonderful Stuff** — 8 East Liberty Street; (912) 238-3279. Nostalgic collectibles. Open Mon.-Sat., 10 a.m.-5 p.m.

• **Kenneth Worthy and James Morton, Antiques** — 319 Abercorn Street; (912) 236-7963. Two floors of English and American antiques and decorative accessories. Open Tues.-Sat., 10 a.m.-4:30 p.m.

• **Youman's Furniture Warehouse** — 314 Williamson Street; (912) 232-7161. Used furniture, bric-a-brac, collectibles. Open Mon.-Fri., 10 a.m.-4:30 p.m.; Sat., 10 a.m.-5 p.m.; Sun., 11 a.m.-3 p.m.

A FEW FAVORITE
TRUNKS AND BLOOMERS

Flowering Plants

• **Azalea** (*Rhododendron*) Evergreen shrub that bursts into color in spring and summer. Many varieties, many sizes, many shades of pink, red, and white.

• **Camellia** *(Camellia japonica)* Rich, glossy green leaves on an evergreen shrub that can become a tree. Blooms in fall and winter in myriad shades of red, pink, and white.

• **Spanish Moss** *(Tillandsia usneoides)* Slender, grey tendrils that shroud trees and fences; actually a member of the pineapple family. Has no roots; absorbs water from humid air; home to red bugs (chiggers).

Trees

• **Crape Myrtle** *(Lagerstroemia indica)* Lovely, ornamental tree; summer blooming in white, pink, red, lavender. Blossoms may stain patio.

• **Dogwood** *(Cornus florida)* A deciduous, flowering tree that grows wild in the woods, showers white blossoms in spring.

• **Chinese Tallow** *(Sapium sebiferum)* A fast-growing, deciduous tree with leaves shaped like Chinese lanterns, "popcorn" seed pods prized by flower arrangers.

• **Live Oak** *(Quercus virginiana)* Georgia's state tree. This hardy slow-grower abounds in Savannah's streets and squares.

• **Magnolia** *(Magnolia grandiflora)* Fragrant, creamy-white blossoms from spring into summer. Lustrous green leaves, attractive fruit cone with red berries.

Vines

• **Wisteria** Japanese and Chinese *(floribunda and sinensis)*, hardy vines that produce fragrant, lavender and white clusters in springtime.

• **Jessamine, Carolina** *(Gelsemium sempervirens)* Native vine with sweet-smelling, yellow flowers that appear in early spring.

EDUCATIONAL AND CULTURAL EVENTS

The Savannah calendar is a fabulous feast of concerts, ballet, theater, films, lectures, classes, workshops, and tours of homes and gardens. Here are some of the organizations contributing to a rich schedule:

Armstrong State College — (912) 927-5211
Beach Institute African/American Cultural Arts Center — (912) 234-8000.
City Lights Theater Company — (912) 234-9860
Historic Savannah Foundation, Inc — (912) 233-7787
Savannah Art Association, Bishop's Court, Trustees' Garden — (912) 232-7731.
Savannah Ballet Theatre — (912) 236-2894
Savannah College of Art and Design — (912) 238-2400
Savannah Science Museum — (912) 355-6705
Savannah State College — (912) 356-2186
Savannah Symphony Society, Inc. — (912) 236-9536
Savannah Theatre Company — (912) 233-7764
School of Visual Arts/Savannah — (912) 651-1280
Telfair Museum of Art — (912) 232-1177

Newspapers and Chamber of Commerce publications have current information.

Calendar of Major Annual Events

January
Martin Luther King, Jr. Birthday Celebration. (912) 234-8000

February
Georgia Heritage Celebration. (912) 233-7787
Black History Month. (912) 234-8000
Telfair Ball and Auction. (912) 232-1177

March
Christ Church/Historic Savannah Tour of Homes and Gardens.
(912) 234-8054
Saint Patrick's Day Festival. (912) 233-4903 or (912) 234-0295
Savannah Onstage Concert Series. (912) 236-5745

April
Earth Day Celebration. (912) 651-6610
Hidden Gardens of "NOGS" (North of Gaston Street) Tour.
(912) 238-0248
Savannah Food Fest. (912) 234-0295

May
Arts on the River Weekend. (912) 651-6417
Lucas Theatre Street Festival. (912) 232-1696
Massie May Festival. (912) 651-7022
Memorial Day Festival. (912) 234-0295 or (912) 238-1779
Scottish Games. (912) 964-4951 or (912) 897-5781

June
Tybee Music Festival. (912) 234-5884

July
Forsyth Performing Arts Festival. (912) 651-6417
Great American Fourth of July Celebration. (912) 234-0295
Savannah Maritime Festival. (912) 236-3959

September
Black Heritage Festival. (912) 651-6417
Savannah Jazz Festival. (912) 236-3414 or (912) 236-2075
Savannah Folk Music Festival. (912) 927-1376

October
Night in Old Savannah. (912) 238-1779
Oktoberfest on River Street. (912) 234-0295
Savannah Greek Festival. (912) 236-8256
Siege of Savannah Observance. (912) 238-1779

November
Coastal Empire Fair. (912) 354-3542
Festival of Trees. (912) 238-2777
Jewish Food Festival. (912) 233-1547
Oatland Island Cane Grinding Festival. (912) 897-3773

December
Holiday Tour of Homes. (912) 236-TDNA
Christmas on the River. (912) 234-0295
Christmas Tour of Historic Inns. (912) 822-4553

For 1996 Olympics information and schedule, telephone SOSCO, (912) 231-1996.

RECREATION

Golf Courses

• **Bacon Park** — Shorty Cooper Drive; (912) 354-2625. 27 holes; public. Open daily, 7 a.m.-8:30 p.m. Rates: Weekdays—walking, $11.75; cart, $21.25; Weekend—walking, $13.75; cart, $23.25. Twilight rates.

• **Mary Calder** — West Lathrop Avenue; (912) 238-7100. Nine holes, semi-private. Open daily, 7:30 a.m.-7 p.m. Rates: Weekdays—walking, $8, cart, $15; Weekends—walking, $10, cart, $17.

• **Sheraton Savannah Resort** — Wilmington Island; (912) 897-1615. 18 holes, semi-private. Open daily 7 a.m.-6 p.m. Rates: $48.10 all year, includes cart.

• **Southbridge** — 415 Southbridge Boulevard; (912) 651-5455. 18 holes, semi-private. Open Mon.-Fri., 8 a.m.-7 p.m.; Sat.-Sun., 7:30 a.m.-7 p.m. Rates: (cart included) Mon.-Thurs., $29.50, Fri.-Sun., $36.

Near Savannah:
• **Callawassie** — off highway 170, between Beaufort and Hilton Head, S.C.; 1-800-221-8431. 27 holes; semi-private. Open daily, 8 a.m.-dusk. Rates: out of season (May 15-Sept. 30 and Dec. 1-Feb. 28) $52 with cart; in season (Mar. 1-May 15 and Oct. 1-Nov. 30) $73 with cart.

• **Cat Island** — 1 Island Causeway, Beaufort, S. C.; 1-800-221-

9582. 18 holes; semi-private. Open daily 7:30 a.m.-6:30 p.m. Rates: $35 all year, with cart.

• **Hilton Head National** — US Highway 278, Hilton Head, S.C.; (803) 842-5900. 18 holes; public. Open daily, 7 a.m.-7 p.m. Rates (cart included) range from $32 to $68, depending on season.

• **Islands West Golf Club** — US Highway 278, Hilton Head, S.C.; 1-803-757-6660. 18 holes; public. Open daily, 7 a.m.-6 p.m. in spring, summer, and fall; 8 a.m.-5 p.m. in winter. Rates (cart included) range from $41 to $62 depending on season.

• **Rose Hill Country Club** — US Highway 278, Bluffton, S.C.; (803) 842-3740. 27 holes; semi-private. Open daily 7:30 a.m.-5:30 or 6 p.m. (8 a.m.-5 p.m. Dec. and Jan.). Rates: (cart included) summer and winter, $35; spring and fall, $40. ($5 less after 12 noon)

Tennis

• **Bacon Park** — Skidaway Road; (912) 351-3850. Open Mon.-Thurs., 9 a.m.-4 p.m.; Fri., 9 a.m.-1 p.m. (After 1 p.m. Sat., courts are unlocked but clubhouse is closed.) 16 lighted courts. Rates: $1.75 per hour in daylight; $2.25 per hour with lights; $10 per hour for ball machine. Call for reservations.

• **Daffin Park** — 1500 East Victory Drive; (912) 351-3851. Six clay courts; three lighted, hard courts. Open daily, 8:30 a.m.-7 p.m. (6 p.m. in winter). Rates: hard courts, free; $2.25 per hour on clay. Call for reservations.

• **Forsyth Park** — south end of park; (912) 351-3850. Four lighted (until 11 p.m.), hard courts; unsupervised, no reservations, free.

• **Tybee Island Community Park** — (912) 786-4698. Two lighted courts.

Bicycle Rental

• **Cyclelogical** — 322 West Broughton Street; (912) 233-9401.
• **Wheelman Bicycle Shop** — 203 West Congress Street; (912) 234-0695.

Boat Charters/Marinas

• **Chimney Creek Fishing Camp** — 40-A Estill Hammock Road, Tybee Island; (912) 786-9857.
• **Hogan's Marina** — 36 Wilmington Island Road; (912) 897-3474.
• **Miss Judy Charters** — 124 Palmetto Drive; (912) 897-4921.
• **Sail Harbor Marina** — 618 Wilmington Island Road; (912) 897-2896.
• **Saltwater Charters** — 111 Wickersham Drive; (912) 598-1814.
• **Savannah Bend Marina** — Thunderbolt, Ga., (912) 897-3625.
• **Tybee Island Charters** — Tybee Island; (912) 786-4801.

Camping

• **Bellaire Woods Campground** — 805 Fort Argyle Road; (912) 748-4000.
• **Rivers End Campground** — Tybee Island; (912) 786-5518.
• **Skidaway Island State Park** — 5 Diamond Causeway; (912) 598-2300.

Hiking or Biking Trail

• **McQueen's Island Trail** — U.S. Highway 80 East (Tybee Road);
(912) 652-6786 or (912) 652-6780.

MEDICAL HELP AND
USEFUL INFORMATION

• **Americare Nursing Services** — 7135 Hodgson Memorial Drive; (912) 350-6200 or (912) 350-6300, with 24-hour "on call." Registered nurses, licensed practical nurses, certified nursing assistants, pediatric and obstetric assistants, physical therapists; medical equipment.

• **Chatham Area Transit (CAT) Bus Service** — (912) 233-5767. CAT's wheelchair-lift-equipped buses are marked (wheelchair symbol). The CAT Bus Book provides schedules.

• **Clark's Professional Care** — 1-800-803-3434. Non-emergency transport for wheelchairs, stretchers.

• **Immediate Med** — 2014 East Victory Drive; (912) 927-6832. Open daily, 9 a.m.-9 p.m.

• **Memorial Family Medical Associates–Historic District** — 232 East Broughton Street; (912) 231-9956 or (912) 231-9869. Mon.–Fri., 8 a.m.–4:30 p.m.

• **Memorial Medical Center** — 4700 Waters Avenue; (912) 350-8390. Full service hospital and trauma center.

• **Physician Finder** — (912) 353-2220. A community telephone referral service at no charge. Call Mon.-Fri., 8 a.m.-8 p.m.

• **Poison Control Center** — 1-800-282-5846. 24 hours a day, every day.

• **St. Joseph's Health Center** — 4704 Augusta Road; (912) 966-2366. Branch of St. Joseph's Hospital; open 7 days a week; call for hours.

• **St. Joseph's Health Center** — Drayton and Henry Streets, near historic district; (912) 232-2003. Downtown branch of St. Joseph's hospital; open 7 days a week; call for hours.

• **Wachtel's, Inc.** — 402 Bull Street; (912) 236-4271, in historic district. Pharmacy, medical furniture and supplies.

Useful Information

Location — Savannah is on the Georgia/South Carolina border, 17 miles from the Atlantic Ocean. Interstate 95 (north-south) and Interstate 16 (east-west) provide automobile access.

Population
Savannah — 150,000
Chatham County — 270,000

Climate — average weather 51 degrees in winter; 66 degrees in spring and fall; 80 degrees in summer. Humidity-72%; Freezing days-32; 90 degree days-66.7; Rainy days-110; Annual rainfall-49.7 inches; Annual snowfall-.1 inch.

Savannah International Airport — from historic district, take I-16 west to I-95 North, exiting at 18A. (Allow at least 35 minutes.)

Airlines
• **Delta** — 1-800-221-1212.
• **Continental** — (domestic) 1-800-525-0280; (international) 1-800-231-0856.
• **USAir** — 1-800-428-4322.

• **ValuJet** — 1-800-825-8538.

Bus Lines
• **Greyhound** — 610 West Oglethorpe Avenue; 1-800-231-2222.
• **Chatham Area Transit** (local) — 900 East Gwinnett Street; (912) 233-5767.

Railroads
• **Amtrak** (passenger) — 2611 Seaboard Coastline Drive; 1-800-872-7245 or (912) 234-2611.

Car Rentals
• **Alamo** — (912) 964-7364.
• **Avis** — (912) 964-1781.
• **Budget** — (912) 964-4600.
• **Dollar** — (912) 964-6080.
• **Hertz** — (912) 964-9595.
• **National** — (912) 964-1771.
• **Thrifty** — (912) 967-2277

Transportation Services
• **Adam Cab** — (912) 927-7488
• **Airport Taxi** — (912) 269-5586
• **Low Country Adventures** (limousine service and shuttle to Hilton Head, S.C.) — (912) 966-2112
• **McCall's Transportation Service** — (912) 966-5364
• **Yellow Cab** — (912) 236-1133
Approximate taxi fare from airport: to historic district, $15; to suburbs, $20; to Skidaway Island, $30.

Driving Distances in Miles to:
Atlanta—250
Charleston—110
Jekyll Island—91
Jacksonville—140

Education
43 public schools and a vocational technical school. Many parochial and independent schools, from pre-kindergarten through high school.
Colleges and Universities: Armstrong State College; Savannah State College; Savannah College of Art and Design; Savannah School of Visual Arts; Savannah Tech; South College; Coastal Georgia Center for Continuing Education.

Government
Savannah: elected mayor, 8 aldermen and city manager.
Chatham County: elected chairman, 8 commissioners and county manager.

Hunting and Fishing — State Game and Fish Division — (912) 651-2221.

Library System — 19 branches of Chatham County Public Library, bookmobile.
Main branch — (912) 652-3600.

THE ARTISTS

Pamela Huber Glendinning (pages 21, 31, 57) grew up in Brazil. She studied gouache, oil painting, and ceramics at the Museum of Modern Art in Rio de Janiero. Later she studied in France and Spain, then served an apprenticeship in portrait painting under Catarina Baratelli in Rio. Since 1986, she has been living and working in Savannah.

Pamela Hanvey Lee (pages 20, 29, 36, 40, 42, 44, 46, 52, 54, 58, 66, 69, 72, 75, 90) earned a degree in Art Education from Florida State University in Tallahassee. She has been an art teacher in public and private schools in Florida and Georgia. A resident of Savannah since 1975, she is known for her line drawings of historic sites and lowcountry scenes.

Lynda Potter (pages 118-119) specializes in watercolor paintings of flowers and landscapes. Following painting studies in high school and at New Paltz State Teachers' College, New York, she studied with more than 20 professional artists. She teaches at the Hilton Head Art League, The County Council of Beaufort, S.C., and the Savannah Art Association.

Leonora Quarterman (page 23) (1911-1979) is well-known for her distinctive watercolors and silk screen prints of Savannah and the lowcountry.

THE MAPS

Robert Scotland Cooper, husband of Emmeline, was born in Atlanta and graduated from the Citadel in Charleston. Since retirement from the U.S. Corps of Engineers, he concentrates on the Cooper Workshop where he restores antiques and builds Renaissance lutes.

FRONT COVER PHOTO

Jack Leigh is a Savannah photographer whose photographs have appeared in numerous magazines, newspapers, art and history museums, and have been published in an ongoing series of award-winning books: *Oystering: A Way of Life; The Ogeechee: A River and its People;* and *Nets & Doors: Shrimping in Southern Waters.*

BACK COVER PHOTO

Robert Scotland Cooper, Jr. is Emmeline's son. He is a graduate of Savannah Country Day School and Georgia Southern University. He is a photographer for the *Statesboro Herald* and also does free-lance photography.

INDEX